Success with

Roses

D1827347

HALINA HEITZ

Series Editor:
LESLEY YOUNG

MEREHURST

Introduction

In many cultures roses symbolize perfect beauty, and what gardener would be really content without at least one rose in their garden? This full-colour guide to rose growing is tailored for the complete beginner but will also offer new ideas to experienced rose lovers. In this book, author Halina Heitz, herself a passionate rose gardener, explains all the most important facts you need to know to ensure problem-free roses that will flower abundantly from summer right through into autumn. A veritable kaleidoscope of roses is introduced here, including attractive, sweetly scented and, above all, robust bedding roses, tea roses, climbing roses, bush roses, old-fashioned rose varieties and English roses, together with ground-cover roses and miniature roses. There is also basic advice on the practical care of roses: planting, pruning, propagating and grafting. Step-by-step illustrations are used to demonstrate the correct way to do these simple tasks and make them easy enough for anyone to follow. The chapter on diseases and pests provides useful full-colour leaf checklists which will quickly help you to identify what is wrong with your roses and eliminate the need to spend ages hunting in other books. In addition to all the gardener's lore, you will also find plenty of ideas and suggestions for planting and positioning roses so that they are shown off to their best advantage, whether in a bed or large container, against a house or garden wall, in an archway or grown as a charming standard rose. In addition, recipes that use roses as ingredients in tea and punch are included, as well as ideas for health and beauty preparations.

Contents

Miniature rose "Bluenette".

Delicate perfection – "Eden Rose 85".

The author
Halina Heitz has written several books on gardening, covering subjects such as palms, orchids and houseplants. For fifteen years, she was editor in chief of a well-known gardening magazine and is a passionate rose grower in her spare time.

Acknowlegements
The author and publishers would like to thank the Federal German rose raisers and rose tree nurseries for their invaluable information and recommendations on varieties; Eckard Riedel, garden architect and head of the gardening department of the council of the town of Lahr in Germany, for his interesting ideas on design; Bernard Mondo, head of the Roserie at the Bagatelle Park, Paris, for his help in classifying roses; also Jürgen Stork and the other plant photographers for their beautiful photographs; and, finally, Ushie Dorner for her very informative illustrations. Special thanks go to garden director Josef Raff, President of the VDR.

NB: Please read the Author's Note on page 63 in order that your enjoyment of this fascinating hobby may not be spoiled.

An enchanting combination of plants – roses and blue larkspur.

Beautiful blooms on thorny stems

What are Floribunda and Polyantha roses, what are dormant buds and what is a grafting point? A short description of the botany of roses will answer all such basic questions and will quickly give you a simple overview of the life cycle of this splendid ornamental plant.

What is a rose?

The botanical name of the rose is *Rosa*. It is included in the family of *Rosaceae* and is actually closely related to apple and cherry trees, *Potentilla*, hawthorn (*Crataegus*) and *Geum*. Nobody really knows how many species of rose there are. There might be 175, or even 400, as the rose is naturally inclined to producing hybrids, which means that one species of rose will cross quite happily with other rose species without any help from humans. Each species includes countless varieties. It is estimated that there are currently more than 20,000 varieties. Roses are included among trees and shrubs as they produce soft, leafy shoots during the summer, which become hard and woody in the autumn. Even when viewed quite soberly, without any poetic licence, the rose can be counted among the most beautiful, resilient and versatile flowering plants we have.

A brief anatomy of roses

Like most other plants, roses consist of roots, shoots, leaves and flowers. Each part of the plant has its own task to fulfil.

The roots support the rose stems or bush and serve to absorb water and nutrients. At first the roots grow very long, then they branch out and, with increasing age, become several metres long and as tough as steel cables.

The crown (or grafting point in a grafted plant) is the thick lump at the neck of the root, at the union of the stock and the scion, which should always be covered with soil, particularly during the winter.

The shoots include all the parts of the rose that grow above ground, both the new, young shoots and the older, woody shoots. In the case of grafted roses, the main shoots grow out of the grafting point, branch out during the summer (annual shoots) and produce a wealth of leaves, from the axils of which numerous flowers appear and grow more profusely every year.

The buds are evenly distributed along the shoot above an imaginary horizontal line. The upper buds are generally fat, look ready to burst and usually produce shoots. The lower buds remain like tiny dots and are therefore called dormant buds. They will form reserve buds for the following year.

The thorns are more or less densely distributed along the shoots and branches and, in some species, even on the undersides of the leaf veins and on the hips (fruits of the rose, see p. 6). They may be fine, bristly or tough, and are coloured red, green, brown or pale yellow. If they are removed from the plant the epidermis of the shoot will not be damaged, all that remains will be an oval mark. Most roses have thorns, although some are only sparsely equipped, while a very few have no thorns at all.

The leaves grow alternately along the shoot and consist of three, five, seven, nine or 15 individual small leaves. The stalk of the leaf is constructed in such a way that the leaf is fairly mobile and is, therefore, protected from the effects of the weather. The leaves help with the transportation of water and are among the most important organs of the plant for absorbing nourishment. They are like miniature factories which extract carbon dioxide from the air and produce organic substances, such as starch and sugar, with the help of light, water and chlorophyll.

The enchantment of a rose arch
A doorway to a magic land may open in any garden as in this rose garden at the Beutig in Baden-Baden, Germany. In the foreground is the white climbing rose "Venusta Pendula".

Shapes of growth

1. Bedding or tea roses can grow up to 40-100 cm (16-40 in) tall. Bedding roses produce several umbel or panicle-like inflorescences; tea roses usually have individual flowers on long stalks.
2. Bush roses spread and grow up to 1-3 m (40-120 in) tall.
3. Standard roses are bedding, tea or climbing roses that have been graft-ed on to a stock. They will attain heights of 60, 90 or 140 cm (2, 3 or 5 ft).
4. Climbing roses produce 1.5-6 m (5-20 ft) long shoots, depending on the variety.

While there are hardly any variations in the shape of the leaves, they can be distinguished according to surface consistency, colour and the shape of the edges. There are shiny, matt, leathery, delicate, smooth, wrinkled, light, medium and dark green, bronze and copper-coloured leaves. The red colouring of the young shoots depends on the species of rose and is thought to be a protection against sunlight. Particularly during the spring, roses store anthozyane (a plant pigment) which protects the plant from being burnt by the aggressive spring sunlight.

The flower is the botanical feature which serves to identify the individual species or variety of rose. It consists of green sepals and petals, male stamens with filaments and the female part (gynaecium) with the style and stigma.

The number of petals varies considerably. Single flowers have less than eight petals, semi-double have eight to 20, double flowers 21-29, and some many-petalled doubles have 30-40 or even as many as 70 or over. The petals can be round,

oval, heart-shaped or wedge-shaped, with wavy or fringed edges.
The shapes of flowers arise from the number of petals. One can find deep-cup, open-cup or shallow-cup flowers, pompons, flat flowers, rosette-shaped, star-shaped and carnation-like flowers (photo, p. 8). The colours of flowers range from white, via all shades of yellow, pink and red to bluish and violet. Pure blue or black roses do not yet exist (see p. 9). Most roses are one single colour, but there are some in two colours, several colours or stripes and even specimens showing only a hint of another colour.

The shape of the flower bud depends on the number of petals and may be egg-shaped, spherical, pointed, slim or urn-shaped.

The fruits of the rose are called hips and, depending on the age and size of the rose and its species, there may be 12-50 hard little pods which contain seeds. Hips come in many shapes: spherical, flattened spherical, pear- or egg-shaped, spindle- or bottle-shaped, and are coloured red, orange, green, brownish-red or blackish-red.

Inside, the hips are packed with bristly hairs, known to many country children as "itching powder" when a hip is broken open and the contents emptied down a playmate's collar! Many roses produce extremely beautiful hips which make an attractive feature in the garden. The fruits of some roses are renowned for their extremely high content of vitamin C. About 100 g (3½ oz) of fresh hips from *Rosa haematodes*, for example, can contain four times as much vitamin C as an orange! In the case of *Rosa rugosa*, the same amount can be obtained from 940 mg; from *Rosa villosa* 920 mg; from *Rosa moyesii* 850 mg. The hips of cultivated garden roses, on the other hand, contain only meagre amounts of vitamins.

The life cycle of the rose
The vegetative phase of the rose begins with the shoots. These appear after the winter rest period, growing from the buds that remained dormant and undamaged throughout the winter. The shoot grows and is initially nourished by nutrients stored in the plant. As soon as the leaves have unfolded, photosynthesis begins to take place in order to supply the plant with nutrients. During this process, carbohydrates (sugars) are made with the help of water and light and carbon dioxide drawn from the air. The nutrients produced in the leaves are transported throughout the inner part of the shoots to all parts of the plant where new tissue is being formed, which is mainly in the shoot and root tips, in the tissue responsible for the thicker growth of the shoots (cambium) and in the parts of the shoots and roots that have already turned woody, where the nutrients are stored. Extracting nutrients from the soil is an equally important process. The very fine, hair-like roots absorb water con-

taining dissolved nutrients and, if required to do so, will absorb a systemic insecticide in the same way. This mixture is then transported through the shoots to the leaves where water is constantly evaporated (through transpiration).

The soil must be well aerated and warm for this process to take place naturally. Further important factors are sufficient moisture in the soil and plenty of nutrients.

My tip: Always keep an eye on the foliage of roses. Lots of healthy-looking leaves are a prerequisite for the good growth of wood and a profusion of flowers. Roses which have produced leaves by the third month of spring will flower earlier.

Grafted roses

Most of the roses grown in gardens are grafted plants. Grafting roses offers two advantages:

1. New varieties can be propagated quickly.
2. An attractive, but naturally weak-growing variety is made stronger through grafting.

In grafting (see p. 56) a budding shoot (or scion) from a chosen variety is grafted on to the neck of the root (the stock) of a particularly robust and healthy species of rose (e.g. *Rosa canina* "Intermis", *Rosa canina* "Pfänders", *Rosa* "Laxa", *Rosa multiflora* and others).

The scion will fuse with the stock and carry on growing. Shoots will grow and the stock and roots will supply the new plant with moisture and nutrients. The grafting point is the most sensitive part of the plant and should, therefore, be covered with up to 5 cm (2 in) of soil.

Different shapes of growth

Obviously, most people who plant roses would like to know beforehand how a particular variety will develop later on – whether it will climb, hang down, creep along the ground, remain low, grow tall, spread out or remain compact. It is often impossible to tell by looking at a bare plant in a nursery what it will look like when it has grown, as plants that are offered for sale have usually been pruned back. Pictures of flowers on packets or tags do not convey much either. The lovely blooms they show could belong to 30-cm (12 in) high dwarf roses or to 2-m (2 ft) high bush roses. Depending on their shape of growth, roses are divided into seven different groups (see table below).

Distinguishing roses according to their history

In most catalogues, different varieties of rose are often not only distinguished according to their shape of growth, but sometimes according to their historical origins.

Very old or old-fashioned rose varieties: Strictly speaking, a rose is classed among the old species or varieties if the class it belongs to was known to exist before 1867, the year in which the first hybrid tea rose "La France" was introduced. Among the most important groups are Gallica, Damask, Portland, Alba, Centifolia (cabbage) roses, Moss, China, Bourbon, Noisette, tea and hybrid perpetual roses. The latter represent the link between the old and modern roses.

Modern roses: This is the name given to the varieties and hybrids which were bred from these groups.

English roses: These are modern roses created by the British rose cultivator David Austin who managed to combine the charm and scent of old roses with the abundance of flowers and vitality of modern roses (see p. 31).

Roses grouped according to their shape of growth

Bedding roses, depending on the variety, will grow from 40-100 cm (16-40 in) tall and bear numerous single, semi-double and double flowers on umbel or panicle-like inflorescences. They are also known as Polyantha or Floribunda roses because of their profusion of flowers.

Tea roses, also known as hybrid teas, grow to about the same height as bedding roses. The main difference between the two kinds is that the flowers of tea roses usually grow singly on long stems, have a particularly handsome appearance and are often scented.

Bush roses are 1-3 m (3-10 ft) tall bushes which will flower once or several times during the summer, depending on the variety.

Climbing and rambling roses, depending on their origins, may grow 1.5-6 m (5-10 ft) long. Both once-flowering and repeat-flowering varieties are available.

Dwarf roses, as a rule, attain a maximum height of 30 cm (12 in) and produce numerous clusters of flowers with small blooms. They are also called miniature roses.

Standard roses and cascade roses do not grow naturally in these shapes but have been created by grafting bedding, tea or climbing roses on to wild stock. May grow up to 60 cm (24 in), 90 cm (32 in) or even 1.5 m (5 ft) tall.

Ground-cover roses creep or form hanging, arching shapes. They rarely grow higher than 80 cm (32 in) but may form shoots up to 2 m (6 ft) long. Some grow upright and, because of their delicate appearance, are often planted between shrubs.

Flower shapes

The appearance and the number of petals give the flower its typical shape. The individual petals may differ considerably: round, elliptical, heart-shaped, wedge-shaped, some with wavy edges, some with smooth edges.

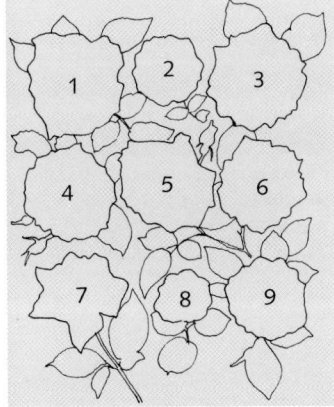

1. A many-petalled variety with 30-70 petals.
2. A double to semi-double flower with 10-12 petals.
3. Flowers with a shallow cup.
4. A flattish flower shape with short, regularly arranged petals.
5. A double flower with more than 20 petals.
6. A single flower with less than eight petals.
7. A classical hybrid tea shape.
8. A globular shape, in which the petals form a sphere.
9. A quartered flower.

Scent

Without doubt, one of the most attractive features of the rose is its beautiful scent. As a rule, dark-coloured roses are more strongly scented than light-coloured ones and roses with numerous, substantial petals have a stronger scent than those with simpler petals. Red and pink roses mostly produce the typical scent of roses, while yellow and white ones may have a scent reminiscent of nasturtiums, violets, lemons or irises, and orange roses may smell of fruit, irises, violets or clover. Other roses smell of ferns, moss, oranges, laurel, honey, wine, lily-of-the-valley, pepper, parsley or even of linseed oil, like Rosa foetida, the Austrian briar rose. A heavier soil will generally engender a stronger scent in roses than a light soil. Roses that have been treated with fertilizer do not develop such a strong scent.

The legendary oil of rose, prized since antiquity, is obtained through distillation or enfleurage. Out of all the presently known roses, there are really only two species that are of major importance for oil extraction.

● Rosa damascena "Trigintipetala" produces the finest and most expensive rose oil of south-eastern Europe, also called attar of roses.

● Rosa centifolia, the cabbage or Provence rose, is cultivated predominantly in the region of Grasse in southern France and produces rose oil for the perfume industry. Rose oil is an orangey-green colour. Thirty roses are required to produce one drop of rose oil and at least 3,000 kg (59 cwt) of flowers are needed to distil 1 kg of rose oil! The oil has a special place in herbal medicine and in the cosmetics industry and is also used to make pot-pourri.

Blue or black roses

The creation of a blue or black rose is a long-held ambition of rose cultivators all over the world but, unfortunately, one that is doomed never to be fulfilled. A blue pigment has actually been found in roses, but it is always bound to a red pigment so that the best one can obtain is a more or less exciting shade of lilac. The crucial factor for blue flowers, the purple pigment delphidin, does not occur in the Rosaceae family. One report from the nineteenth century stated that the Arabs grew blue roses the colour of lapis-lazuli but this later turned out to be a piece of gardeners' trickery. Still, there are a few so-called "blue" roses among the enormous selection of species and varieties. Their colours are variously described as lavender, lilac, violet, mauve or purple. Examples include "Shocking Blue", "Big Purple" (photo, p. 14), "Veilchenblau", "Mainzer Fastnacht", "Charles de Gaulle" (photo, p. 25), "Blue Perfume" and "Nil Bleu".

Equally, the dream of a genuine black rose has never been fulfilled, which is probably just as well as funereal black really would not suit the rose. The well-known British rose expert Jack Harkness is of the opinion that nature refuses to co-operate with the raisers who seek such dark colours because very dark-coloured flowers would be ignored by insects and this, in turn, would endanger the survival of the species. Therefore, let us simply enjoy what nature does allow, such as dark red roses whose flowers remind one of old Burgundy wine, e.g. "Tatjana", "Bakarole", "The Squire" (photo, p. 31), "Black Lady", "Mildred Scheel" (photo, p. 25), "Burgund" and "Papa Meilland".

Roses are true sun-lovers

Roses love a sunny position. If cared for properly, they may flower for up to 20 years in the right spot. Choose the variety and position for planting in with great care. Always make sure the plants are of good quality as, in the long run, it will pay off.

Considerations before buying

There is no doubt that if a rose is planted in the best position, you should have few problems and will derive much pleasure from it. Before planting, check the chosen position for its suitability. The type of soil and the prevailing climate will have a greater influence on the growth, formation of flowers and health of a rose than is generally appreciated. Those of you who have had to dig up a rose because it just did not seem to be thriving, produced few flowers and was practically never free of black spot, will know how very difficult and tedious this job can be. Rose roots grow very deep.

The ideal position for a rose

Roses need light, air and sunshine. They will thrive in any nutrient-rich, well-aerated and water-permeable soil, but why are these factors so important?

Light and sunshine are absolutely indispensable for the development of flowers. Roses need a minimum of five to six hours of sunshine daily. *Air* – not a draught, but a gentle, warm breeze moving through the foliage – will protect the rose from diseases.

Nutrients should be present in the correct ratios for a plant which grows and blooms so luxuriantly. *Water-permeability* is extremely important as roses have deep roots. A layer of impermeable clay or stone underground will obstruct drainage and create problems with the growth of roots.

The following positions are unsuitable:

● positions that have densely packed soil, particularly underground (e.g. the gardens of newly built houses);
● shady positions;
● extremely hot positions. Even though roses are sun-lovers, they like their "feet" to be shady and cool. Heat accumulation along a house wall has a particularly negative effect on rose plants. The roses will fade more quickly and the colours will deteriorate; in some varieties the petals may become burnt;

● positions where there is considerable pressure from the roots of other plants;
● in the corners of walls or thickets of shrubs where air cannot circulate;
● positions where the wind is able to whip trailing branches about and dry them out; as well as draughty, cold positions;
● beds in a hollow. Cold air is heavier than warm air and sinks. In winter this may create frost pockets;
● an extremely acid peaty soil or sandy soil. Do rhododendrons, azaleas, heathers and blueberries grow particularly well in your garden? If so, it is not advisable to plant roses.

Exhausted soil

Never plant new roses in soil in which roses have already been grown for several years. The new plants would soon begin to deteriorate because the soil has become "rose tired". It is believed that the cause of this is an imbalance in the minerals and trace elements in the soil, which has been created through a one-sided absorption of nutrients or through imbalanced fertilizing. In addition, it is assumed that toxic waste products from the old roses' roots remain in the soil and then interfere with the growth of the new roses. Sometimes the soil is also infested with eelworms.

My tip: If you still wish to plant roses in the same place that roses grew before, you will have to dig out the soil to at least a depth of 60 cm (24 in) and replace the "rose-tired" soil with fresh, vital soil from another part of the garden. The exhausted soil should be tipped on to the compost heap. If you add *Tagetes* and *Calendula* to the compost heap, you will find that secretions produced by both of these members of the Compositae family will kill eelworms.

The best soil for roses

The wonderful thing about roses is that they can actually manage to grow on most types of garden soil. None the less, some rough guidelines may be useful.

The ideal soil profile (which means a section cut through the various soil layers), consists of the following levels, according to the famous Swiss rose grower Dietrich Woessner:

● a permeable bottom layer of gravel, pebbles or sand, through which water can run as through a sieve;

● an in-between layer consisting of a mixture of fine particles of rock, silt and clay;

● a thin layer of humus and clay particles;

● a richer layer, 60-80 cm (24-32 in) thick, of loamy and humus-rich agricultural or garden soil. The best type of all is a neutral, fertile loess.

The acid content of the soil is expressed by means of pH values. For roses this should be between pH 6.4 and 7.5, which means that the plants will thrive in a slightly acid, neutral to slightly alkaline soil. In my experience, however, roses will also grow quite adequately in soils with a pH value of 8 or even a little over, as long as the other locational factors are good.

A balanced supply of nutrients means that the main nutrients of nitrogen (N), phosphorous (P) and potassium (K) are present in sufficient quantities. A soil sample will determine this. For this purpose, six to eight spadefuls of soil are dug out at different points in the position where the roses are to be planted. Take a handful from each of these portions, mix them all together and send a 500-g (1 lb) sample of the mixture to a soil analysis expert in a strong plastic bag (ask about this at your local garden centre).

Glass globes will provide a dramatic contrast to the colour of the roses.

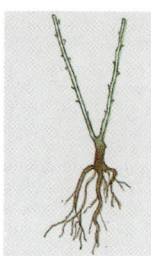

Looking for roses of quality
Plants of the very best quality (left) should have three shoots; roses of lesser quality should have two strong, healthy shoots.

You can also obtain do-it-yourself soil analysis kits which are easy to use at home.

Preparing the soil

You should start to prepare the soil at least three months before planting so that it can settle and mature. Dig the soil over to a depth of 60 cm (24 in). Then loosen the bottom layer of soil with a garden fork and enrich it with organic material (e.g. well-rotted compost or chopped up grass sods). The soil consistency may vary considerably from one part of the garden to another as no two soils are exactly alike. The best way to get to know your garden soil is to test it with your hand. You will soon discover how its structure can be improved. The main types of soil are:

● Clay-rich soil. This soil is heavy, feels sticky and can be formed into a lump. The addition of compost or sand will make it looser.
● Loamy soil is of a crumbly consistency and falls apart easily. If the sand content is very high, the humus content can be increased by mixing in compost. Flakes of various water-retaining materials can be worked in.
● Sandy loam feels grainy and can be formed into a ball more easily. It will generally not need any additional compost etc.
● Acid soil should be improved by mixing in lime.
● Alkaline soils can be improved by working in peat.

A selection of tried and tested roses

(* = flower once; all other varieties are repeat-flowering)

Tea roses
"Carina" – silver pink, 70 cm (28 in)
"Duftwolke" – coral red, 70 cm
"Evening Star" (photo, p. 25) – pure white, 70 cm (28 in)
"Gloria Dei" (photo, p. 25) – creamy yellow/with a hint of pink along the edge, 70 cm (28 in)
"Piroschka" (photo, inside front cover) – pink, 50 cm (20 in)

Bush roses
"Centenaire de Lourdes" (photo, p. 26) – rich pink, 1.8 m (64 in)
"Dirigent" – blood red, 2 m (80 in)
"Lichtkönigin Lucia" (photo, p. 26) – lemon yellow, 1.5 m (60 in)
"Marguerite Hilling" – carmine pink, 2 m (80 in)
"Mozart" – pink/white centre, 1.5 m (60 in)
"Robusta" – red, 2 m (80 in)
"Scharlachglut"* – scarlet, 2.5 m (100 in)

"Schneewittchen" (photo, p. 27) – pure white, 1.2 m (48 in)

Bedding roses
"Bella Rosa" (photo, p. 23) – pink, 50 cm (20 in)
"Bonica 82" (photo, p. 59) – pink, 70 cm (28 in), spreading
"Friesia" (photo, p. 23) – yellow, 70 cm (28 in)
"Ludwigshafen am Rhein" – light red, 70 cm (28 in)
"Märchenland" (photo, p. 23) – salmon pink, 1 m (40 in)
"Manou Meilland" (photo, pp. 52-3) – dark pink, 70 cm (28 in)
"Margaret Merrill" – white/breath of pink, 70 cm (28 in)
"Nina Weibull" – carmine red, 70 cm (28 in)
"Queen Elizabeth" – silver pink, 1 m (40 in)
"The Fairy" (photos, pp. 32, 33) – pink, 70 cm (28 in), spreading
"Tornado" – fiery red, 60 cm (24 in)

Climbing roses
"Flammentanz"* (photo, p. 28) – blood red, 4 m (160 in)

"Golden Showers" (photo, p. 29) – lemon yellow, 2.5 m (100 in)
"Ilse Krohn Superior" – white, 3 m (120 in)
"New Dawn" – delicate pink, 3.5 m (140 in)
"Parade" – dark pink, 4 m (160 in)
"Rosarium Uetersen" – dark salmon pink, 3 m (120 in)
"Sympathy" (photo, p. 28) – dark red, 4 m (160 in)

Ground-cover roses
"Heideröslein Nozomi"* – delicate pink, 30 cm (12 in) tall, 50 cm (20 in) wide
"Palmengarten Frankfurt" – carmine red, 70 cm (28 in) tall, 1 m (40 in) wide
"Repandia"* – pink, 40 cm (16 in) tall, 3 m (120 in) wide
"Rote Max Graf"* – red, 50 cm (20 in) tall, 3 m (120 in) wide
"Snow Ballet" – pure white, 50 cm (20 in) tall, 1 m (40 in) wide
"The Fairy" (photos, pp. 32, 33) – pink, 70 cm (28 in) tall, 1 m (40 in) wide

My tip: While preparing the soil, use this opportunity to remove all weeds with tenacious root systems, like field bindweed *Convolvulus arvensis, Ranunculus repens* (creeping buttercup) and dandelion (*Taraxacum officinale*). This will save a lot of tedious weeding between the rose bushes later on. Leave all small stones in the soil as they will help to aerate it.

Where to buy roses

Roses are among the most popular flowering plants and are therefore almost always included in the standard selection of plants found in the gardening trade. Good sources are:

● Rose cultivators and mail order firms where you can order from a catalogue or buy direct. These firms will obviously have the largest selections (for addresses, ask at your local garden centre).

● Tree nurseries which also sell other shrubs usually have a large selection of roses and will also know about local soil conditions etc.

● Garden centres, whose selection generally represents a cross-section of the best-known varieties.

● Garden mail order firms, whose autumn catalogues generally include a wide selection of roses (ask at your local garden centre for addresses).

Choosing varieties

Like all woody plants, roses are planted at the time of their dormant growth period (the exception being container roses). This means that they have to be bought when they are not flowering, have been pruned back and all look more or less the same. As the flower is the main reason for buying the plant, it is necessary to be clear beforehand about varieties, colours of flowers and other criteria such as the shape of growth, hardiness and common health problems (see pp. 21-33).

How roses are offered for sale

1. As a plant with bare roots, the most usual way.
2. As a container plant. The selection is somewhat restricted.
3. Prepacked in bags, boxes or cartons. The roots are enveloped in moisture-retaining material.

A selection of tried and tested varieties

If you are not sure what you want and have no great experience with roses, it is best to fall back on the sort of list that is compiled by experienced rose growers. The best thing to do in these circumstances is to visit a reputable rose-growing nursery and discuss your requirements with a trained member of staff. If you can tell them as much as possible about the position in which you intend to plant your roses, the kind of soil you have and what your prevailing weather conditions are, etc., they should be able to suggest a suitable selection of plants for you to choose from. If you are unable to visit a nursery, the next best thing is to send off for some catalogues from nurseries recommended to you by your local garden centre. Such catalogues are usually very informative and the choice of plants on offer is usually wide. There is the further advantage that plants from such a source will be healthy and strong so you can get them off to a good start. If you buy plants from supermarkets, traders' stalls or other less-specialist outlets, then you may be unlucky as to quality. Certainly, you are unlikely to receive any reliable advice from non-specialist retailers or their staff.

Looking for quality when you buy

Roses of the best quality should display at least three well-matured branches, of which at least two should be growing out of the grafting point; the third may grow out of the stem above the grafting point (see illustration, p. 12).

Roses of slightly lesser quality should display at least two branches which must both grow out of the grafting point. Things are slightly different if you are looking at standard plants. The prerequisite for the best quality standard roses is shoots with two buds. When buying standards of slightly lesser quality, you should look for one bud. In addition, the height of the standard plant should also be considered. For cascade or weeping types, look for a height of about 140 cm (56 in); for ordinary standards look for plants making a height of 90 cm (36 in); and for miniatures, choose plants with stems of about 40 cm (16 in).

How roses are sold

There is a traditional way of selling roses and three more modern methods.

● Plants with bare roots are most frequently offered for sale just as the tree nusery staff have dug them up (illustration, p. 13). They can be bought individually or in bundles of five or ten. Occasionally, the shoots are treated with a coating of wax to prevent them from drying out through evaporation.

● Plants in plastic bags, boxes or cartons. These are prepacked rose plants whose roots are wrapped in moss or some other moist packing material (see illustration, p. 13).

● Rose plants with a rootstock that is ready for planting.

● Container plants (see illustration, p. 13). These roses stand in plastic pots and are also sold when they are in flower. However, not all roses can be obtained in containers, only the most popular varieties.

When to order and purchase?

This will depend mainly on the planting time. In most regions, autumn is considered to be the ideal time. In very cold regions or if you have very heavy soil, it would be advisable to plant roses during the first or second months of spring. Container roses can be bought and placed out of doors all year round except when temperatures are freezing, but they will grow better if they are planted during autumn or spring.

When buying roses from a catalogue, the following points should be considered.

As a rule, order the plants as early

A scented rose from New Zealand
"Big Purple" is a new 80-cm (32 in) tall tea rose cultivar with large buds and many-petalled flowers.

as possible and always in writing! If you have noted the names of some favourites during the summer months and find them advertised in your catalogue, then send off for them right away. The dispatching of plants is usually done by rose tree nurseries during the middle of the second month of autumn, following the sequence in which orders were received. If you have placed your order early, the plants should be on your doorstep at the ideal time, sometime in the third month of autumn. If you would prefer to plant roses in the spring, you can place your order from the first month of winter onwards. Delivery will be from the first month of spring in frost-free weather.

Standard roses will usually be sent a few days later than other roses during the autumn, as they require longer to prepare.

If you go to pick up the plants yourself, you will be able to buy your roses at short notice without a long wait for delivery time. In the case of rarer varieties, check first to make sure that they are in stock.

Container roses are available all the year round but the selection will probably be at its largest at the typical rose-planting times of the year, in the autumn and spring.

What to watch out for when purchasing roses

A healthy well-grown plant is the first step towards success. A good quality rose should have the following appearance:

● It should have green shoots and a smooth bark.

● The wood should be well matured, and the shoots should feel firm when squeezed.

● The plant should have strong roots.

● Prepacked roses may dry out if they have been allowed to lie around for too long. Check to see

whether the shoots look fresh and green.

My tip: When purchasing container roses, ask if you can look at an example of a plant removed from its pot. You will be able to tell the quality of the container plant by its well-developed rootstock.

Choosing roses

Rose gardens are like shop windows. The most beautiful rose displays, exhibiting the greatest number of varieties, can be found in:

● rose gardens (information can be obtained from the Royal National Rose Society, your local rose growers' society, local tourist office or the Royal Horticultural Society in London (see p. 63);

● parks and public gardens;

● gardens of stately homes etc.;

● at garden and flower exhibitions;

● show gardens of rose nurseries.

My tip: When you go abroad on holiday, keep an eye out for special roses! Many varieties which you might discover in Germany, Switzerland or France will also thrive in Britain and can be ordered from a good rose tree nursery when you get home again, although it may be sold there under a different variety name. If you are a member of a gardening club or rose growing club, you may be able to view roses in private gardens.

Rose catalogues are sent out every year by the big rose tree nurseries. They usually come with photographs in full colour, a detailed description of the variety and valuable tips from experts on how to grow them successfully. Sometimes a small cover charge is made but this is always well worth the expense as every brochure is like a small reference book and the charge is often refunded when a purchase is made.

Roses, herbaceous plants and shrubs

Mixed borders are the kind of garden bed that reflects all that is best about the summer months – roses, herbaceous plants and shrubs. Although the rose is considered by many to be the queen of flowers, it is still very willing to share its space with other plants such as *Campanula*, larkspur (*Delphinium*), catmint and sage. The small-flowered, modern rose cultivars are especially suited to unusual combinations. Their flowers are like scented dots of colour in an impressionist painting.

The planting of colourful "English" beds is popular all over Europe and is an idea frequently employed by garden designers such as the famous garden architect Eckard Riedel, who designed the suggestions for combinations that appear on page 19. However, if you wish to combine shrubs and herbaceous plants with roses you will have to plan your bed very carefully. Only then will the flowerbed do you justice.

Like a painting by Monet
Small-flowered Floribunda roses in shades of pink harmonize beautifully with flowering herbaceous plants and shrubs in the same range of colour or in pastel shades.

Designing a rose bed

Roses will enrich any garden provided that they are positioned in a knowledgeable way. This means not just planting things in any old place without thinking about it first! A few basic principles of good design must be taken into account.

● Never plant tea roses or bedding roses individually. A group of three to ten specimens looks much better.

● Never plant roses together with woody shrubs which will grow higher than the roses and deprive them of light or prevent you from caring for the roses properly. Make sure the root systems of shrubs will not impede the growth of the roses.

● Avoid the close proximity of plants which produce very bright summer colours.

● Instead, use low-growing, sun-loving shrubs with less conspicuous colours or flower and leaf colours which harmonize well.

● Surround roses with a framework of plants like box, lavender or cushions of herbaceous plants in suitable colours.

● Choose backgrounds made of tranquil conifers, green ivy, blue-violet *Clematis*, etc.

My tip: There is a current trend for planting small-flowered, delicate-looking roses in a bed full of shrubs and herbaceous plants. This can look very effective (photo p. 16).

Roses for different purposes

Roses can be used in a very versatile way in gardens and on patios and balconies because of their varying shapes of growth and their wide range of colours.

Bedding and tea roses can be used as a group in small and large beds, together with herbaceous plants, for borders along paths and for use as cut flowers.

Climbing roses can be used as a decoration on house walls, as solitary plants, as climbers along fences, walls, over statues, pergolas, pillars, espaliers and as a background for herbaceous plants and low-growing shrubs.

Once-flowering bush roses can be used as solitary plants to help to anchor banks and slopes, to provide winter food for birds (hips), as part of a natural hedgerow or for opening up a nature garden.

Bush roses which bloom several times a year can be used as solitary plants in open, flowering hedges, as a background for shrubs or herbaceous plants and together with low-growing shrubs or deciduous or coniferous trees.

Miniature roses can be used in borders, for planting in cemeteries, for balcony boxes, containers or troughs and in a rockery.

Cascades or standard roses can be used as solitary plants in a classical, symmetrical garden design.

Ground-cover roses can be used to anchor slopes, banks and shrubberies, for troughs and in a rockery.

Should roses be given an underplanting?

Underplanting should only be done if the roses are well spaced out. The best companion plants to choose are low-growing shrubs and herbaceous plants which can be used as underplanting for climbing roses or bush roses which have become bare below.

Do not underplant roses with bulbs if at all possible. Jobs like digging holes and moving soil will disturb the bulbs and the roses' thorns will interfere when you dig up the bulbs.

Exception: Flowering bulbs which have been allowed to go wild can live under very hardy, older roses or under roses in milder regions, which do not need to be protected in winter by banking up soil.

Making the most of colour in planting combinations

With white roses: plants with green, silver grey and blue grey foliage as well as plants with blue and white flowers.

Examples: box, *Dianthus plumarius* "Diamant", fat hen (*Sedum spurium* "Album superbum"), lady's mantle (*Alchemilla vulgaris*), *Campanula lactiflora*, snow in summer (*Cerastium*), wormwood (*Artemisia*), *Santolina, Gypsophila*, sneezewort (*Achillea ptarmica*), *Stachys lanata* "Silver Carpet".

With red roses: for red shades with a tinge of yellow try plants with blue grey, silver grey, green, brownish-violet and yellowish-green foliage. For red shades with a tinge of blue the ideal flower colours are blue. For red shades with a tinge of yellow try flowers that are orange or golden yellow.

Examples: fat hen (*Sedum album* "Coral Carpet"), *Sedum floriferum* "Weihenstephaner Gold", *Campanula portenschlagiana*, catmint, lavender and larkspur (*Delphinium*).

With yellow roses: with roses in warm shades of yellow try plants with blue, violet, brown red or orange flowers or plants with silvery or golden yellow foliage.

Examples: catmint (*Nepeta*), lavender, *Helichrysum*, thyme (*Thymus rotundifolius*) and *Stachys lanata*.

With pink roses: plants with blue green, silvery or green foliage, as well as inflorescences in shades of violet, purple or blue violet.

Examples: fat hen (*Sedum album* "Coral Carpet"), lady's mantle (*Alchemilla vulgaris*), *Campanula, Polygonum affine* "Superbum", thyme, (*Thymus pseudolanugenosus, Thymus serphyllum* "Coccineus").

Suggested combination 1

Floribunda rose "Sankt Florian" with larkspur (Delphinium belladonna "Völkerfrieden"), Achillea filipendula "Sonnengold", tickseed (Coreopsis verticillata "Grandiflora") and sage (Salvia officinalis "Berggarten").

Suggested combination 2

Floribunda rose "Boys Brigade" with Gypsophila paniculata "Schneeflocke", Potentilla "Goldteppich" or sage (Salvia nemorosa "Ostfriedland"). If you like, you could add a blue element, e.g. Campanula persicifolia "Grandiflora Alba".

Suggested combination 3

Ground-cover rose "The Fairy" with larkspur (Delphinium x cultorum "Sternenhimmel"), catmint (Nepeta faassenii), Capanula carpatica "Chewton Joy", Stachys lanata and lady's mantle (Alchemilla mollis).

Suggested combination 4

Bedding rose "Esther Ofarim" with larkspur (Delphinium x cultorum "Sternenhimmel"), lavender (Lavandula angustifolia "Munstead"), golden rod (Solidago hybrid "Leraft") and phlox (Phlox paniculata "Schneehase").

A selection for your garden

If you have developed an enthusiasm for planting roses, on the following pages you will find illustrations and descriptions of splendid varieties picked from the most popular groups of roses. Choosing will not be easy as they are all beautiful, charming and worth a place in your garden.

The range and possible choice of roses is so enormous that one would need many books filled with photographs and descriptive text to introduce all the many varieties that are for sale today. The following cross-section is intended merely to give you an idea of the great variety of flower colours and shapes. We have taken our selection from the roses most often recommended by raisers – tried and tested varieties selected with the benefit of many years' experience.

Note: Most modern varieties bloom more than once in their flowering season. Roses which flower only once but do so profusely are included. If you wish to use the following illustrations as a guide to choice, you should be aware that you may find variations in colour and shape of flower which can be caused by varying climate or soil.

The sequence of our selection
- Bedding roses, see pages 22-23.
- Tea roses or hybrid tea roses, see pages 24-25.
- Bush roses, see pages 26-27.
- Climbing roses, see pages 28-29.
- Old-fashioned and English roses, see pages 30-31.

- Ground cover and miniature roses, see pages 32-33.

You will find characteristic features listed for every group, plus indications as to their most suitable use and brief details about each individual rose, conveying essential information on growth, height, colour of flowers, scent and other interesting features. With some groups of roses there are additional recommendations on variety, e.g. scented flowers or those with particularly attractive hips.

Special recommendations

By means of a questionnaire, a survey was carried out among rose growers, which asked them to make recommendations of particular varieties for certain purposes. Some of the results are given below.

Roses for planting on steep slopes: The most suitable are bush roses which are not too high and ground-cover roses.
Examples: "Fair Play, "Fiona", "Fleurette", "Heidekind", "Heidekönigin", "Hermann Schmidt", "Immensee", "Max Graf", "Palmengarten Frankfurt", "Red Meidiland", "Red Yesterday",

"Repandia", "Repens Meidiland", "Rote Max Graf", "Sommerwind", "Super Dorothy", "Super Excelsa", "Swany".

Roses for screening
Examples: "Bischofsstadt Paderborn", "Castella", "Ferdy", "Feuerwerk", "IGA 83 München", "Lichtkönigin Lucia", "Queen Elizabeth", "Robusta", Rosa rugosa and hybrids, "Rosika", "Royal Show", "Schneewittchen", "Shalom".

Roses with few thorns are found mainly among the greenhouse roses which are used for cut flowers
Examples: "Bonica 82", "Karl Höchst", "Kronpinzessin Viktoria" (no thorns), "Madame Sancy de Parabière", "Montana", "Sutter's Gold".

Roses for flower arrangers
Examples: "Alliance", "Berolina", "Bonica 82", "Carina", "Carmen", "Corso", "Desiree", "Diadem", "Flamingo", "Kardinal", "Konrad Henkel", "Kristall", "Lady Rose", "Landora", "Mabella", "Majolica", "Marlies", "Monica", "Pascali", "Prominent", "Queen Elizabeth", "Rouge Meilland", "Rumba", "Sutter's Gold", "Tatjana", "The Fairy", "Träumerei", "Uwe Seeler".

Roses that are resistant to traffic exhaust fumes (for planting along busy roads)
Examples: "Alba Meidiland", "Anne Cocker", "Bonica 82", "Centenaire de Lourdes", "Dagmar Hastrup", "Fanal", "Flammentanz", "Max Graf", "New Dawn", "Red Meidiland", *Rosa nitida*, *Rosa rugosa* hybrids, "Sarabande", "Swany", "The Fairy".

Cascades of flowers
The much-loved, but not very resistant, "Dorothy Perkins" is now available without a susceptibility to mildew under the name "Super Dorothy".

Most beautiful in groups

Bedding roses

Depending on the variety, bedding roses can grow from 40 to 100 cm tall (16-40 in) and will produce numerous single, semi-double or double flowers with umbel-like or panicle-like inflorescences. They are also called Polyantha or Floribunda roses because of their profusion of flowers. They are used in beds, together with shrubs, in borders along paths and as cut flowers.

"Traumerei" growing in a box-edged border.

Scented bedding roses
White: "Margaret Merill"
Yellow: "Arthur Bell", "Friesia"
Red: "Duftwolke", "Ludwigshafen am Rhein", "Prominent", "Traumerei"
Pink: "Elysium", "Manou Meilland", "Pariser Charme"

"Apricot Nectar" blooms well into the autumn and has 10-cm (4 in) wide, large double flowers. This bushy-growing Floribunda rose has dark green foliage and grows up to 90 cm (32 in) tall. It has a wonderful scent.

"Lilli Marleen" is considered to be one of the most beautiful dark red Floribunda roses. Its open, double, cup-shaped flowers are about 8 cm (over 3 in) across. This rose flowers profusely, grows bushy and will grow up to 60 cm (24 in) tall. Its foliage is bright green and resistant to disease.

"Friesia" belongs among the top class yellow roses and is often used in mixed borders together with shrubs (see p. 19). It grows up to 65 cm (26 in) tall, upright and bushy and has fresh green, shiny leaves. The deep yellow, semi-double flowers do not lose their colour, are strongly scented and fade neatly. Particularly hardy.

"Bella Rosa", a Kordes cultivar from the 1980s, enchants with its giant umbels of double flowers in glowing pink. The petals unfold from rounded buds and release a scent of wild roses. This variety has won countless gold medals. It grows up to 60 cm (24 in) tall and sports fresh, green, shiny foliage. Its compact, bushy growth makes it an outstanding bedding rose.

"Märchenland" is notable out for its extraordinary resistance to disease. The flowers of this variety, which grows up to 100 cm (40 in) tall, are salmon pink, large and semi-double, the leaves are medium green, matt and leathery. This rose grows strongly and spreads. Suitable as a small bush rose.

"Lavaglut" produces rounded, black red buds which turn into double, blood red, very rain-resistant flowers. It grows up to 60 cm (24 in) tall and spreads. The foliage is dark green and shiny.

Tea roses and hybrid teas

These roses are particularly enchanting on account of their generally strongly scented flowers which are large and handsome and usually grow individually on long stems. Tea roses or hybrid teas grow, on average, from 50-100 cm (20-40 in) tall, are bushy and very upright and look particularly attractive in small, exclusive groups or in the company of shrubs with silvery green foliage. Of all the groups of roses, they provide the most elegant cut flowers. We recommend pinching out the lateral buds early on in order to obtain large single flowers for cutting. The range of colours extends from white through cream, champagne, pink, salmon pink, orange and red to such unusual colours as blue violet, burgundy or black red.

Tea roses in two colours

"Caribia" (photo, p. 42), "Circus Knie", "Die Welt", "Königin der Rosen", "Las Vegas", "Monica", "Neue Revue", "Piccadilly", "Rebecca", "Wimi".

Black red tea roses

"Bakarole", "Black Lady", "Burgund", "Erotika", "Ingrid Bergmann", "Oklahoma", "Papa Meilland".

Blue and violet varieties

"Big Purple" (photo, p. 14), "Blue River", "Charles de Gaulle" (photo, p. 25), "Mainzer Fastnacht".

"Susan Hampshire": The parents of this 80-90 cm (32-36 in) tall, strongly scented hybrid tea rose are the pink to salmon pink variety "Monique", the carmine pink, large flowered "Symphonie" and the famous "Maria Callas" – also known as "Miss All-American Beauty". This very successful cultivar from the famous French rose-growing family of Meilland was first introduced in 1974 and produces densely packed, deep pink flowers from outstandingly large buds. The foliage is a fresh green shade and grows robustly. When planted in a bed, they look best and most elegant in small groups, perhaps framed by box.

"Mildred Scheel": A deliciously scented rose with large, black red buds which gradually open into velvety red, double flowers. This strongly growing hybrid tea rose, also known by the name "Deep Secret", branches out well and forms very tough stems with matt, dark green leaves. It grows to 70 cm (28 in) tall.

"Evening Star", which was created from the hybrid tea rose "White Masterpiece" and the Floribunda rose "Saratoga", displays 10-cm (4 in) wide double flowers in umbels on long, branching stems, and enjoys particularly good health for a white variety. This 1-m (40 in) tall hybrid tea, with its dark green, shiny foliage, grows well and has a strong scent.

"Konrad Adenauer": This 60-cm (24 in) tall hybrid tea, with its clear, velvety dark red, strongly scented blooms, is a creation by the well-known German rose raiser Mathias Tantau. It grows bushy, branches well and possesses extremely healthy, light green foliage.

"Chicago Peace" has double flowers in two colours, consisting of 50-60 petals, and grown on very strong stems. The foliage is deep green and the plant spreads. It can grow up to 70 cm (28 in) tall.

"Charles de Gaulle": The variety "Mainzer Fastnacht" gave this hybrid tea its attractive lilac shade, and the delicious scent originates from "Prelude". This is a vital, strongly growing 60 cm (24 in) tall rose from France with tough, resistant foliage.

"Gloria Dei" is the most frequently bought and most prize-winning rose in the world. This 1-m (40 in) tall, strong-growing hybrid tea has giant, 15-cm (6 in) wide, many-petalled, yellowish-pink blooms and shiny green foliage. It is considered a symbol of joy and peace and is often sold under such names. It was named on the very day, in 1945, when peace was proclaimed in Europe.

Bush roses

Bush roses grow up to 1-2 m (40-80 in) tall and, depending on the species or variety, flower once or several times. While the once-flowering roses (seen growing wild or in parks) are often used for stabilising slopes and embankments, as part of a natural hedgerow, for producing a crop of rosehips and for interspersing among other plants in an organic or rustic garden, gardeners also like to use the modern cultivars, which bloom often (ornamental bush roses) as solitary plants or as effective backgrounds for shrubs or herbaceous plants. Bush roses that only flower once still possess all the charm of wild or botanical roses and are becoming ever more popular as design elements in the planning of natural-looking gardens. **NB:** Do not give everlasting flowering roses a spring pruning. It will be quite sufficient to clear out the dead, old or withered wood.

Solitary roses for small front gardens
"Angela", "Blossomtime", "Centenaire de Lourdes", "Kordes Brillant", "Märchenland" (photo, p. 23), "Mountbatten", "Rosika", "Schneewittchen" (photo, p. 27), "Yesterday".

Attractive rosehips
Rosa canina, Rosa moyesii, Rosa pendulina "Bourgogne", Rosa rubiginosa, Rosa rugosa, Rosa sweginzowii "Macrocarpa", "Scharlachglut".

Once-flowering bush roses
"Conrad Ferdinand Meyer", "Dornröschen", "Frühlingsgold", "Hansa", "Maigold", "Marguerite Hilling", "Pink Grootendorst", "Red Nelly", Rosa nitida, "Scharlachglut".

"Lichtkönigin Lucia" is a profusely flowering, long-lived, outstandingly robust and healthy bush rose. The lemon yellow, 8-cm (over 3 in) wide double flowers grow partly singly, partly in clusters of several flowers and are slightly scented. This rose grows at a medium rate, is upright and can reach up to 1-2 m (40-80 in) tall. The leaves are dark green and shiny.

"Centenaire de Lourdes" is a French variety with handsome, open, double, glowing pink flowers of about 8 cm (over 3 in) in diameter. The foliage is shiny green and healthy, growth being a little lanky. Height: about 1 m (40 in). It is also sold as a Floribunda rose.

"Westerland" appears to the observer rather like a flickering burning bush when it is in full bloom. The large, open, double flowers have a strong scent and appear right up until the first frost. The foliage is dense and deep green. This rose grows quickly, is spreading and can attain a height of 1.5-2 m (60-80 in).

"Golden Wings" will even grow in positions that are a little shady, will attain a height of about 1.5 m (60 in) and bears 12 cm (under 5 in) wide, sulphur yellow, single flowers throughout the entire summer. Particularly conspicuous are the orange red stamens which look like gold threads. The leaves are light green and matt. This Rosa spinosissima variety is very hardy but tends to produce suckers from its roots.

"Schneewittchen" is one of the most popular pure white bush roses. It is very dainty in appearance and grows to only about 1 m (40 in) in height. Its 8 cm (over 3 in) wide, double flowers grow densely together, appear until the first frost and stand out beautifully from the shiny green foliage. This rose is sometimes sold under the name of "Iceberg".

"Bischofsstadt Paderborn" is a medium-fast-growing rose, can be grown in smaller gardens and is often planted as a hedge. This rose produces a fine display of semi-double, cup-shaped flowers in a particularly glowing shade of red. It grows to a maximum height of 1.5 m (60 in). The leaves are red at the shooting stage and turn medium green later on.

Rosa moyesii: Whether pink, red or white, roses of the *Rosa moyesii* group always provide an eyecatching feature, even though they flower only once profusely and then display only an occasional flower here and there. At flowering time, the ordinary *Rosa moyesii* is simply smothered in blood red, single flowers which later develop into glowing red rosehips. The white "Nevada" (photo above) flowers equally as profusely. The pink variety, "Marguerite Hilling", is just as beautiful. It creates a real firework display of colours as early as the last month of spring, and will flower a little again in the autumn. Height: up to 2 m (80 in). Foliage: matt green, dense.

Tall roses with masses of flowers

Climbing roses

This group of roses produces splendid drifts of flowers and can attain a height of up to 6 m (20 ft). Climbing roses spread their enchantment over everything: house walls, embankments, stone walls, fences, statues, pillars and espaliers. Both once-flowering and continual-flowering types, with or without scent, are available. Climbing roses that have been grafted onto standards are particularly popular as their flowers appear to cascade down like a waterfall.

In principle, climbing roses are not suited to growing on very exposed south-facing walls as they are in danger of getting burnt by the sun, the colours of the flowers may bleach out and there is an increased susceptibility to attack by spider mites. As long as the base of the plant is kept shady and plenty of water is provided, however, some robust varieties may manage in such a position and not suffer from fading colours.

Robust climbing roses
"Colonia", "Compassion", "Dortmund", "Flammentanz", "Ilse Krohn Superior", "New Dawn", "Parade", "Super Dorothy" (photo, p. 21), "Super Excelsa", "Sympathy".

Scented climbing roses
"Casino", Compassion", "Coral Dawn", "Goldfassade", "Ilse Krohn Superior", "Lawinia", "Morning Jewel", "New Dawn", "Parade", "Rosanna", "Sympathie", "White Cockade".

"Sympathie" is a perpetual-flowering rose with large, very double, velvety red flowers. It grows fast, produces robust shoots and is therefore ideal for training against house walls or over pergolas or arches. The flowers do not lose their colour and will emit a pleasant scent of wild roses. Height: 3-4 m (10-14 ft). Foliage: deep green and shiny.

"Golden Showers" forms flowers which are 12 cm (under 5 in) across, semi-double, light golden yellow which turns lemon yellow as they fade and are grown singly or in clusters at the ends of shoots. The leaves are medium green and shiny. Strictly speaking, it is not a genuine climbing rose but rather a bush rose with shoots which grow 2-3 m (7-10 ft) long.

"White Cockade" is a handsome, creamy white climbing rose with 10-cm (4 in) wide, handsomely formed double flowers which have a strong scent. This rose grows fast and forms shoots up to 2.5 m (over 8 ft) long. The medium green leaves are shiny.

"Flammentanz" was created out of a *Rosa rubiginosa* hybrid and *Rosa kordesii* and is an improvement on the old "Paul's Scarlett Climber" which was once commonly grown all over Europe. This once-flowering rose grows in a spreading pyramid shape, has lots of foliage and is very hardy in frosty conditions. The flowers are glowing red, medium large and double. Height: 4-5 m (14-16 ft). Leaves: matt, dark green.

"Dortmund" has been popular for more than 30 years. Its blood red, single flowers, which hang in luxuriant umbels from strong shoots up to 3 m (10 ft) long, seem to glow because of the white "eye" in the centre. The leaves are small and shiny. This plant is particularly effective as a free-standing bush rose.

"Intervilles" is a luxuriantly flowering climbing rose which can be utilised in different ways. It can be used to cover the trunks of old trees and will make a splendid display scrambling over espaliers or pergola beams or turning fences into a fiery sea of flowers. "Intervilles" was introduced by Robichon in 1968. It flowers more than profusely and right through until the first frosts, displaying glowing, semi-double flowers. Height: 2.50-3.50 m (8-12 ft). The foliage is green and healthy. Other, equally profusely flowering climbing roses include "Blaze Superior", "Flammentanz", "Parkdirektor Riggers", "Rote Flamme", "Santana" and "Sympathie".

Old-fashioned and English roses

These two groups have something in common even although they were created a century apart. They possess all the charm and poetry of the roses we admire in old paintings and tapestries. The main difference between the two groups is that the modern English roses flower more often, a trait rarely found in the old-fashioned species and varieties. Twenty years ago the British rose grower David Austin realized that nostalgia for old roses could help to bring about a spectacular come-back for the old *gallica*, *damascena* and *centifolia* roses with their subtle colours, magnificent scent and beautiful double flowers. He incorporated these old-fashioned roses in his hybridizing work and came up with some astonishing results: roses that look like ancient roses but enjoy all the advantages of modern roses – robust good health, weather hardiness and continual flowering. In addition, he was able to extend the range of colours by several nuances which did not hitherto exist: apricot yellow, golden yellow and salmon pink.

At the present time, some 40 different English roses are available on the market. Most of them do not grow a great deal during the first two to three years, but then make up for it. They do not grow quite as tall as their ancestors and are thus extremely suitable for modern gardens which are, unfortunately, becoming smaller and smaller.

"Gros Chou de Hollande" is also referred to as a Bourbon rose or a *centifolia* in rose catalogues, probably because this very old rose is difficult to categorize. It is well worth growing for its large rose red flowers with an alluring scent. Height: just under 2 m (80 in). Once-flowering.

"Charles de Mills" is an enchanting *gallica* rose with conspicuous dense, many-petalled, scented, burgundy red flowers, 8 cm (over 3 in) across. This upright, fast growing bush can attain a height of 1.5 m (60 in). Once-flowering.

"Madame Isaac Pereire", a Bourbon rose dating back to 1881, grows more than 2 m (80 in) tall, and produces very double, scented flowers in a lovely shade of purple pink. This fast growing plant forms shoots that are well armoured with thorns and has large leaves. It will require some protection during the winter.

"Leda", a damask rose, was created before 1827. It is also known by the name "Painted Damask" and is sometimes seen to flower more than once. The buds are reddish-brown on the outside. The milky white petals are edged with carmine, densely packed in globular, double flowers and have a wonderful scent. Height: up to 1.5 m (60 in). Deep green, large, elliptical leaves. Hardy in frosts.

"The Squire", with its carmine red flowers, is considered to be one of the most beautiful of the English roses. The very large, many-petalled flowers possess a delectable scent. The colours do not fade in the heat and the petals bear up well in heavy showers. The foliage is dark green. Height: 1.2 m (48 in).

"Königin von Dänemark", also known by the names "Belle Courtisane" or "Naissance de Venus", flowers once only but in profligate splendour. In good years for roses the branches hang down almost to the ground due to the weight of the blooms. This rose is the offspring of *Rosa alba*, probably crossed with a damask rose in 1816. "Königin von Danemark" grows robustly and open and may be up to 1.8 m (6 ft) tall. The shoots are strong and frost resistant; the foliage dark, almost blue green. The densely packed, many-petalled flowers, first carmine pink, later much paler, emit a scent of wild roses.

"Charles Austin", an English rose, comes in a rather rare shade that goes very well with the colours of old roses. The very large, apricot-coloured, double flowers smell of fruit. This plant grows robustly, is bushy and can attain a height of 1.5 m (5 ft).

Small, low-growing and versatile

Ground-cover and miniature roses

The ground-cover roses produce shoots up to 3 m (10 ft) long, generally do not grow higher than 80 cm (32 in), creep, grow prostrate or very arched, and rapidly form luxuriant carpets of flowers. Important: do not plant them too close together, otherwise they will force each other to shoot upwards by their third year because of a lack of space and will then lose their

"The Fairy" grows spreading, compact and slightly overhanging.

attractive low-growing habit. Miniature roses flower equally profusely and will also remain low, at a maximum of 35 cm (14 in) in height. In contrast to ground-cover roses, they grow very slowly, so they are very suitable for planting in roomy balcony boxes or tubs.

"The Fairy" produces masses of small flower umbels with double flowers in a very light shade of pink. The delicate shoots branch profusely and soon spread out. This is a robust, healthy rose with small, shiny leaves, which grows to about 70 cm (28 in) tall. Suitable both as ground cover or as a very small bush rose.

"Swany" is a 40-cm (16 in) high, small bush rose with swan white, 4-6 cm (1½-2⅓ in) wide, beautiful double flowers. It grows well and spreads out its long, prostrate or arched branches. Spacing between plants should be 1 m (40 in). The foliage is dark-green and shiny. Very attractive in a front garden and as a cascade on stone walls or gentle slopes.

"Fairy Dance" develops into a carpet during its first year and displays a mass of flower clusters with small, dark red individual flowers. During the second year the branches begin to hang down and will grow to 50-60 cm (20-24 in) long, with shiny foliage.

"Lutin", a charming miniature rose from France, grows no more than 25-30 cm (10-12 in) tall and flourishes in pots. Its light pink flowers are many-petalled and scented. Also known as "Rosa Gem".

"Orange Meillandina" was introduced in 1980 by Meilland and is eminently suitable for pots and balcony boxes but also looks good as an edging around a border. This 30-40 cm (12-16 in) high miniature rose displays 4-cm (under 2 in) wide, large, signal red, double flowers and is noted for its healthy, medium green, slightly shiny leaves. It also comes as pink "Lady Meillandina" and salmon pink "Pink Meillandina".

"Baby Maskerade" stands out on account of its unusual, attractive colouring. The open, double flowers are orange yellow with copper red edges. This miniature rose grows upright and bushy, has matt green, thick foliage and is resistant to diseases and pests. Height: 40-50 cm (16-20 in).

Lots of tender care – and pruning

Roses are not always easy to look after. They require attention and care but you will then be rewarded with a splendid display of flowers which often last all summer long. Looking after roses is a relaxing hobby and one of the best ways of countering stress.

Tools for the rose gardener

With the exception of a special fork for digging, most of the tools needed are the ordinary ones used in the garden:
● a spade and garden fork for preparing the soil;
● a claw-rake for scraping away banked-up earth and for loosening the soil;
● a two-tined rose fork for loosening the ground where plants are close together. This is the best tool for minimizing damage to the roots of the roses;
● well-sharpened secateurs;
● branch cutters with long handles, which can cut through thick branches up to 4.5 cm (approx. 2 in) in diameter;
● a knife for digging out weeds;
● a watering can or garden hose;.
● spraying gear for use with pest control agents and plant care agents;
● a grafting knife;
● gardening gloves for protection against thorns.

The ideal planting time

Roses with bare roots can be planted in the autumn or spring, while container roses can even be planted in the summer. The second and third months of autumn are considered the best time for planting roses in most regions. In regions with rougher weather or where the soil is heavy, it is preferable to plant from the first to second month of spring. Planting methods vary in only one detail: if the roses are planted in the autumn, the shoots should not be cut back until the spring or else they may freeze during the winter. The most important consideration is that the soil should be frost-free, fairly dry and should have been loosened or prepared.

Planting roses

Never, ever add any kind of mineral fertilizer to the soil at the first planting. Fertilizing should not be done until six to eight weeks later, when the rose plant has developed a sufficient number of fine hair-like roots.

Planting roses in containers

Low-growing Floribunda roses, miniature roses and slow-growing ground-cover roses are most suitable (see p. 32). The container should be equipped with drainage holes and be at least 50 cm (20 in) deep and equally wide so that the rose will have enough soil to develop a proper root system. A larger container would be even better. Before filling the container with compost, place a 5-cm (2 in) thick drainage layer of gravel, sand, Hortag or coarse polystyrene flakes in the bottom of the container. The compost should be bought ready-mixed or composed of loamy garden soil mixed with a little peat and sand.

Roses for large containers and boxes: "Alba Meidiland", "Baby Maskerade (photo, p. 33), "Bassino", "Bonica 82" (photo, p. 59), "Friesia" (photo, p. 23), "Guletta", "Heinzelmännchen", "Ingrid Weibull", "La Sevillana", "Nozomi", "Red Yesterday", "Rosmarin 89", "Schneewittchen" (photo, p. 27), "Swany" (photo, p. 33), "Vatertag", "Zwergkönig 78".

Watering

Roses should only be watered until they have developed a proper root system. Always water according to the principle of better once very well than three times superficially. After two to three years you will no longer need to water your roses (except during unusually dry periods, in very dry positions or in sandy soil). Before watering, loosen the soil around the stem a little and then water the root area abundantly.
Warning: Do not wet the leaves when watering as this will promote the formation of sooty mould. Also avoid wetting the leaves of your roses with the lawn sprinkler.

"Raubritter" only flowers once in high summer but then it displays an almost profligate splendour of blooms.

Hoeing

In the spring, after taking away any winter protection from your roses and removing the banked-up soil, it is time to hoe the surface of the soil all around the roses. This will enable air, warmth and moisture to penetrate the deeper layers of the soil. You should also hoe before and after every watering, as well as after thundery downpours and, of course, whenever weeds start growing. We recommend using a two-tined rose fork for dense plantings of roses, as this will make the job a lot easier without damaging the roots. Hoeing is also very beneficial in late autumn.

You will not need to hoe so often if you use mulch.

Mulching

Mulching means laying finely chopped organic material at the plant's "feet". This is quite an easy job to carry out if you have free-standing bush roses. Mulching will smother the growth of weeds, keep the soil moist and encourage the development of beneficial micro-organisms in the soil, which produce humus and thus provide the plants with additional nutrients. It will not, however, replace fertilizing! Suitable materials: dried lawn clippings, chopped straw and well-rotted manure. The ideal mixture is one consisting of both coarse and fine particles. The best time to start mulching is in the spring after removing the banked-up soil, hoeing and fertilizing. In the autumn, you can work this material, which by now will have decomposed, into the soil you use to bank up the roses.

Planting

Planting roses with bare roots

Remove any packing materials from the roses. If the plants have been delivered during a period of frosty weather, they should be allowed to thaw out slowly in a cool room.

1. Water the roses a few hours before planting them; the grafting point (the thick "lump" beneath the branches) should be immersed in the water.

2. Cutting back: remove all damaged roots to avoid danger of decay and shorten any long ones to about 20 cm (8 in). Cutting back the roots makes planting easier and encourages the formation of the fine roots that absorb water. Simultaneously, prune above-ground shoots – not too much if you are planting in autumn, more if planting in spring. This cuts down on surfaces that will lose water through evaporation and the rose will retain more strength for the formation of new roots.

3. Dig a hole deep and wide enough to accommodate the roots comfortably and to enable the grafting point to end up about 5 cm (2 in) below the surface of the soil. If the roots appear to grow mainly in one direction, do not dig a round hole but make it oval. Hold the rose plant in the hole and spread out the roots on a small hillock of soil.

4. Add a mixture of soil and compost until the hole is filled loosely. Then press the compost down firmly (or carefully tread it down), until a neat gulley for watering is obtained.

5. Water this depression several times with plenty of water which will help to wash the soil close to the roots.

6. When the water has drained away, shovel in the rest of the soil and check the position of the grafting point once again.

1. Allow the rose plants to soak for several hours before planting.

2. Remove damaged roots and shorten long ones to 20 cm (8 in).

3. The grafting point should end up about 5 cm (2 in) below the surface.

4. Fill the hole with planting compost and gently press it down.

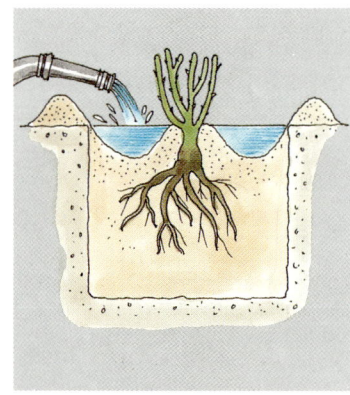

5. Provide the roots with plenty of water.

6. Pile up loose soil to protect the shoots from frost and sun.

Surround the shoots with a "mole-hill" of banked-up soil to protect the rose from frost, sun and wind.
NB: Plant waxed roses in the same way.

My tip: Plants which arrive when the soil is frozen or covered in snow should be put in a bucket of damp sand or soil and placed in a frost-free place (e.g. a cellar or shed). As soon as the soil is frost- and snow-free, you can plant out the roses.

Planting roses in containers
Water the plant thoroughly. Make the hole for planting large enough so that a hand's width of space is left all around the inside of the container. Remove the plastic cover or pot from the plant but do not prune the plant.
Loosen the surface of the rootstock a little. Stand the rose in the hole so that the top of the rootstock is level with the surface of the soil. Fill up the spaces with a soil and compost mixture. Press the compost down well and water the plant thoroughly.

Planting standard roses
Around 95% of standard roses are sold with bare roots, the rest having well-developed root systems in containers. The method of planting will depend on the type of standard you have purchased. In any case, the support post should be driven into the planting hole beforehand. After that, place the rose plant next to it, leaving a space of about 5-8 cm (2-3¾ in). After planting, pressing down and watering (see p. 36), tie the rose to the support post with figure-of-eight-shaped loops. Protect the stem from pressure at the tie by inserting a piece of rubber or sacking.

My tip: It is a good idea to have treated the support post some weeks beforehand with a plant-

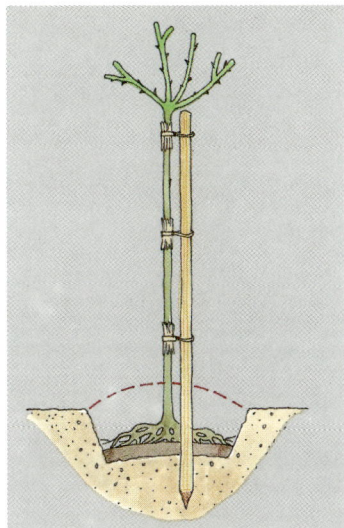

7. Drive in a support stake before planting a standard rose.

friendly wood preservative. Plastic sticks are particularly durable (available in the gardening trade).

Planting climbing roses
Both the size of the hole for planting and the cutting back of the plant are done in the same way as for the usual planting method (see p. 36). If you intend to grow the rose on a wall espalier, dig the planting hole 20 cm (8 in) away from the wall so that the roots will not run the risk of drying out. Lay the roots in the hole at an angle so that the above-ground shoots bend towards the ties. The grafting point should still be 5 cm (2 in) below the surface of the ground. Shovel in the soil-compost mixture, press it down and water the plant thoroughly. Water often during the first year.

If you cannot plant the rose right away
In this case, you should heel the roots into the soil in the garden.

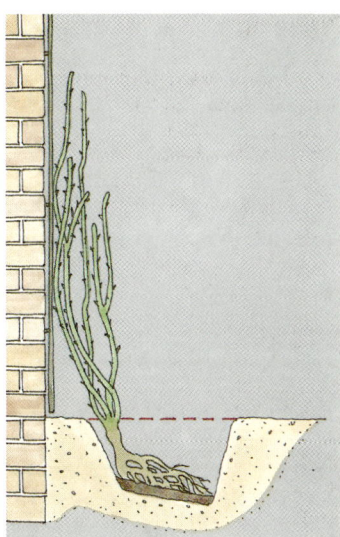

8. Climbing roses should be planted leaning towards their support.

Choose a shady, sheltered spot and dig a slanted hole, lay the rose in it, cover it with soil, then water well. Roses in containers should be placed in the shade and watered.

Spacing between plants
● Bedding and tea roses: 7-10 plants per square metre (10.75 sq ft).
● Miniature roses: 10-12 plants per square metre.
● Ground-cover roses: 1 plant per square metre.
● Climbing roses: require a wall surface area of 15 sq m (160 sq ft). For espaliers, a distance of 3 m (10 ft) should be left between plants.
● Standard and cascade roses: a distance of several metres should be left for appearance's sake.
● Bush roses: will require 1.5-7 sq m (16-75 sq ft) for optimal development, depending on the species and the variety.

Climbing, supporting and espaliers

Climbing roses can produce shoots up to 6 m (20 ft) long. As they do not possess any tendrils or other organs for clinging, they have to be given help and support. The classic rose arches, made of fired zinc, for use free-standing or for leaning against a wall, can be bought in the gardening trade. Various arches can also be placed together to form pavilions, double arches and arcaded walks. In addition, there are numerous other possibilities, e.g. rose arches made of hard PVC or other plastics, cascade rose supports, support fences and espalier kits for driving into the ground, T-espaliers and pyramids. There is always the alternative of building your own individual rose espalier or frame out of treated wooden battens.

Fertilizing

Plants which grow as fast and flower as abundantly as roses should be very well supplied with nutrients. This is done by fertilizing and is all the more important if the roses have been growing in the same place for some time. Freshly planted roses should not be fertilized until they have been established for a while.

Like all other plants, roses need nitrogen (N) for growing leaves, phosphorous (P) for producing flowers and potassium (K) for ripening wood. They also need calcium and silicon to strengthen their tissues as well as iron and magnesium for synthesizing chlorophyll.

Head in the sun, feet in the shade
Herbaceous plants and shrubs planted beforehand will prevent the soil from drying out too quickly.

Which type of fertilizer to use

It does not matter much in what form the rose receives these nutrients. There are different types of fertilizer to choose from.

Organic fertilizer, like ripe garden compost, nettle brew or other plant brews, horn or bonemeal, or well-rotted manure, promotes the development of useful micro-organisms in the soil and thus encourages the formation of humus. However, such materials often contain too much nitrogen and cannot be regulated properly. As it often takes months until they are broken down sufficiently to be available to the plants, they can be spread on the soil in the autumn/winter.

Mineral fertilizers, also called NPK fertilizers, are immediately available for the plant's use. These are applied in the spring when they are required for shoot formation and the growth of leaves (apply in the amount of 70-80 g or 2½-3 oz per square metre).

Organic-mineral fertilizer is also applied in spring (about 120-150 g or 4¼-5¼ oz per square metre).

Further notes on fertilizing: The ideal situation is if it rains after fertilizing. In dry weather, plenty of watering will be required or the fertilizer may "burn" the roses.

If you apply organic-mineral fertilizer to your roses after the beginning of the last month of summer, the roses will remain for far too long in their vegetative phase and this will prevent the shoots from becoming woody and hard, which is extremely important for the hardiness and health of the plant. It is preferable, during the first month of autumn, to work 30-50 g (1-1¼ oz) per square metre of magnesium sulphate loosely into the soil around the roses. This will encourage the wood to form properly before the winter.

My tip: I always combine organic and mineral fertilizing. During the spring I work one handful of mineral or organic fertilizer per plant into the banked-up soil. At the first sign of flowering, the roses should receive another equal dose. After that I observe a strict fertilizer rest period. In late autumn I apply well-rotted compost to my plants.

Indicator plants

Indicator plants are generally referred to as weeds and only germinate in particular soil conditions. However, they are not 100% reliable as they sometimes invade untypical terrain.
- Indicators for nutrient-rich soil that is good for roses: scarlet pimpernel (*Anagallis arvensis*), dog's mercury (*Mercurialis perennis*), stinging nettle (*Urtica*), chamomile (*Matricaria chamomilla*), speedwell (species of *Veronica*), fumitory (*Fumaria officinalis*), wild radish (*Raphanus raphanistrum*) and tufted vetch (*Vicia cracca*).
- Places where the following grow naturally are unsuitable for roses: corn mint (*Mentha arvensis*), mare's tail (*Hippuris vulgaris*) and colt's-foot (*Tussilago farfara*).

Pruning roses

The effect of pruning

Roses flower on the young wood, i.e. on shoots which emerge from buds in the spring. The fattest buds sit right at the ends of the shoots. They start developing first, forming leaves and later flowers. The smaller buds further down remain dormant and will not start to develop until later on. This means that the more you cut back, the longer you will have to wait for buds. On the other hand, cutting back does encourage the formation of new shoots. Cutting back also promotes long life, a willingness to flower and the health of the rose plant.

The main pruning of roses is done in the spring, after removing the banked-up soil (see maintenance cut, right, and p. 41).

Repeat-flowering roses should also be pruned regularly during the summer. When the first flowering is over, you should remove the remains of the flowers but not the healthy-looking buds below them (the best one is the thickest bud in the leaf axil of the second leaf under the inflorescence). This encourages a second flowering.

Once-flowering roses should not be cut back after flowering as they will often produce attractive rose-hips.

Some tips on pruning

Crushed or torn shoots, as well as parts that have not been cut off cleanly, can be a source of invasion by all manner of diseases. For this reason you should only use the very sharpest scissors and secateurs. Make sure that the cut part of the plant is not dirty. If the cut branch or shoot is thicker than a pencil, it is advisable to paint over it with a tree sealant. Diseased or infested shoots should be cut back to healthy wood. Healthy wood is recognizable

Remove all suckers
Suckers grow from the stock below the grafting point. Remove some of the soil and, if possible, cut off the sucker as close to the root as possible.

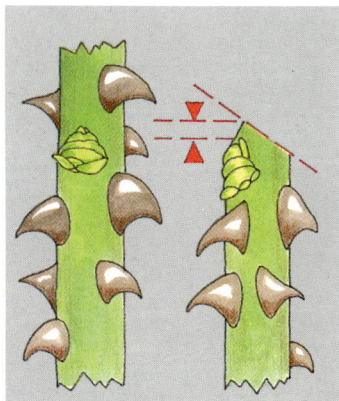

The right way to prune
Cut off the shoot 3-5 mm above an outward-facing bud.

by its white pith; diseased wood has brown pith.

The planting cut

Shorten the above-ground shoots when planting or moving plants. Cutting back in this way reduces the surface area that is exposed to evaporation and allows the plant to retain more strength for the formation of new, fine, water-absorbing roots. When planting in the autumn, cut back sparingly, but in the spring cut back radically, leaving only a few buds on the outsides of the stems.

The maintenance cut

This should take place during the first or second month of spring when the buds begin to swell. (If you wish, you can start cutting back long, lanky shoots in the autumn.) In principle:

● It is best to cut too little than too much. Radical cutting back always results in fewer flowers.

● Allow thick shoots to remain longer; weak or thin ones can be cut back further.

● Old, diseased, dried up, crossing or dense wood should be removed.

● Only cut away the faded flowers of continual-flowering varieties (see left column).

My tip: Minor injuries cannot be avoided when cutting roses, in spite of the protection of gloves. Disinfect open wounds immediately with a suitable remedy from your first aid kit. If you deal with roses on a frequent basis, you should make sure you are protected by a vaccination against tetanus.

Continual-flowering bush roses

(see illustrations 1 and 2)
Frozen, withered or dense wood and shoots which grow sideways

should be thinned out. Lightly cut back shoots from the previous year and, if necessary, cut back thin shoots to three or four buds.
Exception: Do not cut once-flowering roses. Only very old wood which bore hardly any flowers the year before should be removed. This will rejuvenate the plant.

Continual-flowering climbing roses

(see illustrations 3 and 4)
Old, withered wood can be cut back to just above the ground. Shoots which grow diagonally should be removed. New, strong lateral shoots should be cut back to two to five buds. Overhanging shoots should be tidied and tied back.
Exception: With once-flowering roses, pruning should take place immediately after flowering so that the young shoots can grow strong before the autumn. Flowering shoots branching off from healthy main shoots can be cut back to three to four buds. Old wood should be removed just as with continual-flowering climbing roses.

Bedding and tea roses

(see illustrations 5 and 6)
Shorten the shoots by about a third. Cutting more radically will produce longer-stemmed flowers for use as cut flowers. If this is what you want, you should cut back weak-growing varieties to 10-15 cm (4-6 in) and medium-growing varieties to 15-25 cm (6-10 in).

Standard roses

(see illustrations 7 and 8)
Cut back shoots to about 15-20 cm (6-8 in) so that a beautiful round crown is produced. Later, pinch out the new leaves to about three leaves so that the crown becomes bushy.

1. Dead wood which is densely packed should be cut out.

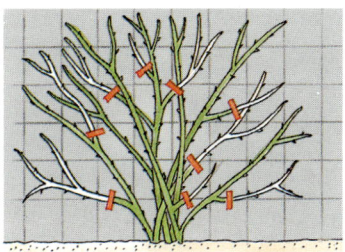

3. New lateral shoots should be shortened to two to five buds.

5. Shorten shoots by about a third and remove crossing shoots.

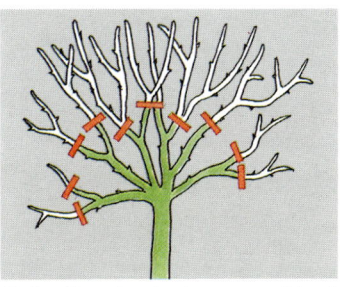

7. Pruning standard roses: cut back the shoots to 15-20 cm (6-8 in).

2. Shoots from the previous year should be shortened.

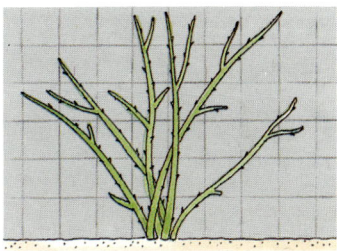

4. Dead wood and crossing shoots must also be removed.

6. Cutting back more radically produces long-stemmed flowers.

8. Later, shorten the shoots to three leaves per shoot.

Balcony roses overwintering in an earth pit
Dig a large pit. Line it with polystyrene sheeting. Stand the rose boxes in the pit and cover them with leaves and brushwood.

Overwintering young standard roses
Bend the rose downward. Protect the stems with conifer branches and fix them to the ground with pieces of wire. Cover the crown with soil.

Protection in the winter

Most roses (apart from wild roses which, without exception, are all hardy) are grateful for winter protection. Before beginning to bank up the soil and wrap your roses up in the last month of autumn, remove all the fallen leaves from the ground (in which, for example, the spores of sooty mould like to overwinter). Any leaves still left on the shoots should be cut off. Then bank up the soil around the stem of the rose plant to a height of about 20-30 cm (8-12 in). Suitable mediums are compost, well-rotted manure or soil. On no account use peat as it absorbs water and would work like an icepack when the temperature drops below freezing!

Tea roses should also be given protective packing using material such as conifer branches which will shield them from agressive winter sun and drying winds.

Climbing roses should also receive extra protection by tying layers of fine conifer branches over them. Climbing roses on posts etc. should be enveloped in brushwood, straw or sacking. Tie up the shoots beforehand!

Standard roses are particularly at risk as their grafting point is situated immediately below the crown. Younger standards (see illustration above) are best loosened from their support, carefully bent over towards the ground (if necessary, loosen the roots a little) and then fixed in position with crossed sticks. The crown (remove the leaves because of the risk of decay!) should be covered with soil. In the case of older specimens which can no longer be bent over, envelop the plant from the crown right down to below the grafting point in conifer branches, sacking or straw. Do not use plastic sheeting!

Balcony roses should not be left outside in winter as the small amount of soil in the container will not be sufficient to protect the roots from the cold. They should be overwintered in a frost-free room (cellar, garage, shed, attic) or sunk in a flowerbed. For this purpose, dig a sufficiently large pit and line it with polystyrene sheets or thick cardboard. The roses should be pruned first, then placed in the pit still in their tubs and covered with straw, thin twigs, dry leaves and/or conifer branches (see illustration left). The soil removed from the pit should be banked up all around the edge of the covering to secure it, but not on the covering itself! In the spring, the tubs are retrieved from their winter quarters and placed in a bright, but not sunny position so that they can begin shooting. If night frosts are forecast, take them inside again!

Removing the winter protection

Towards the end of the first month of spring, the conifer branches can be removed but do not remove the banked-up earth until no more late frosts are expected, generally around the second month of spring. Standard roses should not be straightened up again immediately, but should be left lying for several days after removing the covering. They can then be carefully straightened up, the loosened roots should be firmly pressed down and the standard stem tied back to the support post with figure-of-eight-shaped loops.

A charming two-coloured rose
When planted in a group, this compact and low-growing tea rose "Caribia" produces the effect of a sea of flame.

Romantic climbing roses

This house in Tuscany looks as if it
has been uninhabited for a long
time. The roof tiles are crumbling,
the rendering is cracked, the cur-
tains are closed. In winter it must
look quite forbidding. In the last
month of spring, however, these old
roses transform the ancient walls
into Sleeping Beauty's castle with
their abundance of flowers! Only
climbing roses are able to achieve
such an attractive wall covering with
their long shoots. This rose might
be "Paul's Scarlett Climber" which
forms 6-m (20 ft) long shoots thickly
beset with faintly scented, scarlet
clusters of flowers. This variety of
climbing rose has been planted
throughout Europe since 1916 and
is still very popular. It stands up to
wind and weather with vigour and
displays its timeless beauty, just like
the old house itself.

Climbing roses in Tuscany
*This unknown variety (presumably
"Paul's Scarlett Climber") is so
robust that it will not fade on house-
walls in brilliant sunlight.*

Pests and diseases

Prevention is better than cure

Ladybirds form a first defence against aphids but are not always able to dominate these pests and then it becomes necessary to spray the roses. Nevertheless, if the right type of protection is used in the right position, the rose will usually be resistant to all attackers.

Just as there are no humans who never, ever catch a cold, there are no absolutely resistant roses. This is because of the multitude of environmental factors which affect the rose in any given position. Some varieties thrive particularly well in a certain area but will barely survive in another environment. Some enjoy excellent health for many years and then suddenly become sickly as if they had exhausted all their strength. It is not always possible to find out the causes of poor health. Still, several things can be done to protect your plants from harm.

Precautionary measures
First of all, if you are not quite certain that you are able to offer your roses the very best growing conditions, you should settle for robust roses (see recommendations, p. 12). These roses have been tested under adverse conditions and will put up with a great deal. Further measures which may help to render the use of plant protection agents unnecessary or at least minimize their necessity, are:

● the right variety for the right position;
● good preparation of the soil (see p. 12);
● balanced fertilizing, which should cease at the correct time;
● correct care (pruning, working the soil, winter protection);
● careful observation;
● planting accompanying plants whose emanations tend to ward off pests and fungi, e.g. nasturtiums, garlic, lavender, marjoram, *Tagetes*, wormwood, ornamental chives and onions;
● the avoidance of monocultures (too many roses or Rosaceae in one position).

Warning: In the case of gardens of newly built houses, one is inclined to forget that the soil may have become densely compacted and hard deeper down because of the action of caterpillar vehicles, excavators, etc. Roses which are planted on top of this will rarely thrive and will tend to look sickly as normal water percolation has been considerably disrupted and the roots will become diseased.

Soil samples: Before planting, bore several holes 50 cm (20 in) deep in the position where you intend to plant, and fill them with water. If this has not drained away within an hour, the subsoil will have to be loosened up and improved (see p. 12) or drained.

Method: Dig a 60-cm (24 in) deep trench along the entire length of the flowerbed. In this, lay a plastic pipe with plenty of perforations in such a way that it leads downwards away from the bed. (If this is not possible, the standard method of loosening the soil will have to be employed.) Fill the trench with 5 cm (2 in) of gravel. Afterwards, the roses can be planted or replanted. If the roses have just been dug up, cut off any decayed roots and shorten the shoots. If more than half of the roots are damaged, the roses should be replaced with new ones.

Controlling pests and diseases
In principle, the sooner methods of controlling pests and diseases are implemented, the more effective they are and the less the healthy development of the rose will suffer. Pests and diseases can be controlled in various ways:

Chemically: with insecticides and fungicides and other substances which ward off harmful pests.

Biologically: with plant and mineral plantcare agents and fortifying agents (oils and essences, plant extracts, algae preparations). Also with useful insects.

Mechanically: by collecting beetles, caterpillars, infested leaves, etc. by hand and by cutting out diseased shoots and webs. By scratching off and spraying down infested parts of plants.

Warning: All plant protection agents should be kept out of reach of children and pets.

Employing useful insects

If you find masses of ladybirds crawling about on your roses, it is a sure sign that aphids are present. Aphids draw ladybirds as a delicious banquet draws a gourmet. If you are lucky, their appetite will be sufficient to wipe out the aphids. Very often, however, they cannot cope with the sheer numbers and then spraying becomes necessary. What kills aphids, unfortunately, also kills ladybirds.

Recipes for plant-fortifying agents

The following three plant brews have been used very successfully on roses by organic gardeners.
Mare's tail brew: Soak 200 g (7 oz) dried leaves (obtainable from herbalists) in 10 litres (2¼ gal) water for 24 hours. Boil for an hour. Allow to cool and strain. Dilute it as 1 part brew to 10 parts' water and drench the roses fortnightly with this concoction to fortify their tissues and as a prevention against fungal infections. Mare's tail can also be obtained as an extract in the gardening trade.
Garlic brew: Chop up 10 cloves of garlic and boil them with 2 litres (3 pt) water. Allow to cool and dilute with ten times the amount of water. Spray the roses weekly with the brew. Do not forget to spray the soil beneath! Also spray if the rose is diseased. Garlic contains fungicides and antibacterial sulphur compounds which are still effective even when extremely diluted.
Fermented nettle brew: Allow 1 kg (2¼ lb) fresh nettle leaves or 200 g (7 oz) dried leaves (from health food shops and herbalists) to ferment in 10 litres (2¼ gal) rainwater for two weeks.

What can be read in the appearance of leaves

Damage caused by the climate and mistakes in care

Frost damage: wavy, blistery leaves with spots and brown edges. The cause is late frosts. Leaves which are still growing are particularly at risk.

Sunbun: these spots are caused by watering the leaves in full sunlight. The drops of water act as tiny magnifying glasses. Not a fungal disease!

Waterlogging, also car exhaust fumes and herbicides, will cause this damage in which the leaves display large yellow patches spreading from the stalk of the leaf.

Dryness: leaves which turn yellow in irregular patches and suddenly drop off indicate that the soil has dried out.

Acid burns are caused if some of the grains of mineral fertilizer land on wet leaves. Young shoots are particularly at risk.

What to do

Damage to the leaves causes the rose to lose vital surface area that is required for the assimilation of sunlight. Damaged leaves – with the shoot if necessary – should be removed to encourage the formation of new leaves. In the case of waterlogging, the plant should be dug up and the hole carefully drained. Diseased roots and crown should be cut back carefully and the rose – even if it is the middle of the growth phase – should be replanted. If the weather is extremely dry, water the plant once, very thoroughly and plentifully, then loosen the wet soil.

Symptoms of deficiency

Nitrogen deficiency: The symptoms are sickly-looking shoots, slender, pale green leaves which drop off early and, occasionally, lots of little reddish dots.

Potassium deficiency: The young leaves shine reddish-brown, the older ones have brown edges, the leaves remain small. Often occurs on sandy soil.

Phosphorous deficiency: Young, dark green leaves with purple spots on the undersides and early fall of leaves are symptoms of this problem.

Chlorosis (pale leaves): The absorption of iron needed for the synthesis of chlorophyll is hindered by a high content of calcium compounds in the soil, waterlogging and damage to the wood. Only the veins in the leaves remain green.

Magnesium deficiency: The leaves display yellowish-red, dead areas in the centre of the leaf. Older leaves fall off first. The synthesis of sunlight by chlorophyll is impaired.

What to do

If there is a deficiency in the most important plant nutrients like nitrogen, phosphorous and potassium, rapid relief should be provided by using a fast-working mineral fertilizer or a special rose fertilizer which, as a rule, will also contain the necessary trace elements. If magnesium is missing, magnesium sulphate can be worked into the soil. If chlorosis is displayed, fertilizing the leaves with iron chelates or plant tonics will help. If chlorosis was caused by damage to the wood, the yellowing shoots should be cut back to healthy wood, and then nitrogen-based fertilizer should be given – but only until the first month of summer.

Stir daily until the brew has stopped producing foam.

Dilute as 1 part brew with 10 parts' rainwater. Combat the smell of fermentation with valerian flower tincture which can be mixed in with the brew.

The correct way to spray

Roses, and particularly their young shoots and leaves, often react very sensitively to chemical plant protection agents. This means that the following points need some consideration:

● Any insecticide or fungicide should be suitable for roses, so ask an expert for advice.

● The doses should be correct. One way to be sure is to use dosing devices which enable the gardener to measure out even the smallest quantities.

● Any brew used for spraying should be distributed as a fine spray and should be dry before darkness falls.

● Do not use the sprays too close to the plant.

● Follow all advice given by the manufacturer with respect to toxicity, risk to health and the protection of groundwater and bees for the sake of the environment. Insecticides which are dangerous or not dangerous to bees, as the case may be, should state so on the packaging.

● After using spraying devices, clean them meticulously with water, adding a squirt of washing up liquid. Do not allow rinsing water to run away into the mains sewage, use it for watering!

My tip: The dosages of plant protection agents are often indicated as a percentage. The gradations on measuring beakers etc. vary, giving grammes (g), millilitres (ml) or cubic centimetres (cm³), although all these measurements are exactly the

Changes in leaves due to fungal infections

Black spot: Cool nights after rainfall favour this condition. The star-shaped dark spots will appear from the second month of summer onwards, often even on young wood. Consequence: loss of all leaves.

Powdery mildew: This covers leaves, shoots and buds with a grey white, powder-like film. Cause: unbalanced fertilizing, warm, dry air.

Rose rust: Pinhead-sized blisters on the undersides of the leaves, containing orange red dust (spores of the fungus) which then turn black from the last month of summer onwards.

Leaf spot disease: This occurs more often in damp positions. The leaves are covered in variously shaped spots. If the infestation is severe, total loss of leaves may result.

Sooty mould: This fungus colonizes the sticky secretions (honeydew) of aphids and scale insects and forms a dirty black film.

What to do

Fungal infections seldom disappear by themselves. The causes are not always poor care or a tendency inherent in the variety. Varying weather conditions from year to year play an important role too. If the roses are extremely badly infested, it is worth removing all the leaves in the autumn, even from the ground. In the spring, spray the plant and the ground with mare's tail brew and garlic brew (see p. 47) or with a non-toxic fungicide (ask in your local garden centre). In the case of an acute infestation with black spot, mildew or other fungal infections, try repeat spraying with fungicides specifically formulated for roses. Sooty mould fungi will not disappear until the aphids have been eliminated.

same. Convert as follows:

- 0.02% means 0.2 g/ml/cm³ plant protection agent to 1 litre (1¾ pt) water;
- 0.6 g/ml/cm³ to 3 litres (5¼ pt) water or 2 g/ml/cm³ to 10 litres (2¼ gal) water;
- 0.1% means 1 g/ml/cm³ plant protection agent to 1 litre (1¾ pt) water, 3 g/ml/cm to 3 litres water or 10 g/ml/cm to 10 litres water.

Changes to the buds

Decaying buds are caused by a *Botrytis* fungus which may also infest leaves and leaf stalks. Control: remove all infested parts.
Nibbled buds: This is caused by an insect. Control: not necessary as the problem only occurs sporadically.
Holes made by insects feeding: Control: not necessary as the problem occurs only sporadically.
Stunted buds: The cause is thrips. The buds do not completely unfold and become crippled. Control: cut off infested parts and spray with an insecticide.

Changes in the shoots

Blind shoots: These are caused by insects (e.g. gall midges). The shoot stops growing and does not form any flowers. Remedy: cut the shoot back to the next healthy buds.
Deformed shoots: Two or three shoots grow together by becoming flattened. The cause is thought to be a hormonal disturbance. Remedy: not necessary, as the general growth is not affected.
Cracks in the bark: Caused by frost, radical pruning or overfertilizing with nitrogen. Remedy: damaged shoots should be pruned in the spring.
Tumours: These are caused by bacteria which invade or are accidentally introduced and are then able to develop due to an unfavourable position.

Control: remove infested parts immediately. Spray frequently with garlic brew to strengthen the plant. If necessary, replant the rose in completely fresh soil.

Scale insects: These sit underneath whitish-yellow to brown waxy scales and live off the sap of the leaves. Control: scratch them off, or spray with special oil (ask at your garden centre) in the case of severe infestation.

Withering shoot tips: The cause is the rose borer (*Ardis*) whose larvae bore into the pith. Control: immediately cut back infested shoots and branches. The eggs are located at the shoot tips and base of leaves! Paint the cut surfaces with tree sealant. Repeatedly spray the plant with insecticide.

Changes to the flowers

Red to brownish spots on the petals: This is caused by long-term rainfall. The flowers are unable to dry off and develop spots. Best prevention: choose varieties which are known to be rain-resistant for regions with much rain. Avoid positions which are not well-aired. We recommend immediately cutting off spotty roses in order to encourage the formation of new flowers.

A rose bud appearing out of a rose flower: This phenomenon was once a source of wonder to Goethe! A new shoot grows out of the centre of the rose. This happens more often in small-flowered varieties and is no cause for alarm. Just cut them off.

Tattered petals: Either a feature of the variety or caused by hungry insects like earwigs. Take immediate steps to control the problem.

Damage caused by salt

Rose beds which are situated in front gardens near to a pavement are often at risk in winter from salt strewn to prevent people from slip-

Changes in leaves caused by pests

Owlet moth caterpillars: The clutches of eggs deposited on the top sides of leaves do not harm the plant. However, once the caterpillars have emerged, you have a potentially harmful situation. The caterpillars hide in the flowers and eat the petals.

Leaf wasp: Its green larvae, 6-10 mm long, turn the leaves into skeletons. Often buds and shoots are eaten too. In some years infestation is particularly severe.

Sawflies: This seems to occur suddenly. The feeding canals on the uppersides of the leaves are caused by the larvae. Infested leaves drop off prematurely.

Aphids: Roses are infested by greenfly. They damage the young shoots, buds and leaves, which become crippled. Cause: warm, dry weather.

Small rose-leaf wasp: The wasp, which grows up to 5 mm long, lays its eggs along the edges of the leaves, which then roll up into tubes and are no longer able to function properly.

What to do

Depending on the degree of severity, remove the leaves, pinch off the egg clusters, cut away webs, collect the beetles and caterpillars or wash the aphids off with a strong stream of water. If none of this helps, repeatedly spray the plants against biting and sucking insects with insecticides, meticulously following the manufacturer's directions (ask for products specifically formulated for roses).

Warning: Do not spray during flowering time with agents that are toxic to bees. Repeat the treatment according to the manufacturer's directions as one treatment alone will not eliminate the "rearguard" action of these pests.

ping in icy weather. The full effects are not noticed until the spring. The symptoms of soil that is polluted with salt vary greatly and include falling leaves, crippling of parts of plants, discoloration of the leaves and impaired growth. A great deal of rainfall may dilute the concentration of salt in the soil and it will also help if the water is able to run off into deeper layers of the ground.

Damage by wildlife

If you live in the country or at the edge of a town near a wood or fields, you may find yourself confronted by damage such as nibbled buds. Rosebuds and fresh green shoots are a regular delicacy for deer. If the garden is not fenced in, the only thing to do is to employ substances which drive off wildlife by their odour. These agents are sprayed on the plants or old rags are soaked with them and then hung at a height of 75 cm (30 in), spaced about 5-6 m (16-20 ft) apart, near the roses. Please try to make sure that these agents are non-toxic to bees.

Some agents may not be used in areas where the groundwater is protected by law.

Where else to find advice

If you just cannot figure out what is the matter with your roses, you can turn to your local rose growing club or write to the troubleshooting column of a gardening periodical. You should receive an answer within a fortnight if you enclose a stamped, self-addressed envelope.

Changes in leaves due to pests

Vine weevils will often consume leaves, shoot tips and buds overnight, without leaving much. The larvae are worse as they even gobble up the roots.

Leaf-cutting bee: Holes and irregular chunks eaten out of young leaves point to this pest. This damage generally occurs in the spring and is usually only sporadic.

Red spider mites: The worst rose pest. They suck the sap out of the leaves until they wither and drop off. Plants in extremely hot, sunny positions are most at risk.

Rose cicada: Light-coloured, winged, jumping insects which suck the sap from the leaves and cause whitish-yellow spots. They occur more often in dry, warm positions.

Rose tortrix moth: At first, a small, brownish caterpillar appears, which nibbles at the leaves and petals and then spins webs on the leaves where the larvae form chrysalises.

What to do

The measures described on page 50 will help.

My tip: Vine weevils can now be controlled using biological methods such as nematodes (eelworms) which can be ordered through the gardening trade. The best time for this treatment is the end of the first month of autumn to the middle of the second month, or from the end of the second month of spring to the beginning of the second month of summer, always in the evenings. The larvae-consuming nematodes require sufficient moisture in the soil for their development and soil temperatures of more than 12°C (54°F). This method will be unsuccessful in cold weather. Obviously, you do not wish to create an infestation of nematodes so you must implement such a method with care.

Pink roses are everyone's favourite

When leafing through a rose catalogue, it seems that, after red, pink
is the most frequent colour for
roses. Pink appears in countless
shades, ranging from silver rose to
baby pink, apricot pink, shocking
pink, coral pink right across the
palette to deepest purple. One
might even say that pink is the
characteristic colour of the entire
genus and deeply entrenched in its
genetic programme. It is known that
very many wild roses, the ancestors
of our modern varieties, have flowers in shades of pink: *Rosa gallica*;
Rosa rubiginosa – the sweetbriar or
eglantine rose, *Rosa rugosa* and
Rosa canina – the dog rose, just to
name just a few. The colour pink is
predominant among the old-fashioned roses and even in modern
cultivars. The new English roses by
David Austin display lovely pastel
shades that have never been seen
before. "Trier 2000", the youngest
prize-winning Kordes cultivar, has
pink flowers, as does "Manou
Meilland" (photo, right), demonstrat-
ing that this colour will always
appear in evermore fascinating new
variations in the future.

*One variety – many shades of
colour*
*Whether in bud, half open, com-
pletely open or almost faded, this
bedding rose "Manou Meilland",
with a delicate lemony scent, displays a different shade of pink at
every stage.*

The rose grower's ambition

What would you do if you discovered a rose which is thought no longer to exist in the garden of a friend? Perhaps you would like to grow extra roses of a particular variety. It is not impossible to propagate your favourites. The simplest method is from cuttings – the more tricky one is by grafting.

Roses can be propagated in different ways:
- from seeds;
- from shoots growing out of roots;
- from shoots which hang down and take root (layering);
- from cuttings (see p. 56);
- by grafting (see p. 56).

Propagating from seed

This is only possible with wild or pure species roses which have not been grafted, in other words, whose splendid flowers are derived from the same stock as the roots. As most cultivated roses are grafted, they cannot be propagated from seed because the new plants that would grow from the seed would look nothing like the one you had intended to propagate. Propagating from seed is only carried out if one wishes to obtain a robust and healthy stock for grafting purposes. These "wild plants" can be obtained from tree nurseries. The best known grafting stocks come from varieties of the dog rose, *Rosa canina* "Intermis" and "Pfänders".

Propagating from shoots

This is only possible with roses which produce long, trailing shoots, for example, *Rosa nitida*, *Rosa omeiensis* "Pteracantha", *Rosa rugosa* and its varieties "Alba" and "Hansa", *Rosa spinosissima* (Scotch rose or burnet rose) as well as *Rosa gallica*.
The long shoots can be chopped off with a sharp spade and planted in the desired position.

Propagating from hanging shoots which take root (layering)

Roses with pliable branches are suitable for this method. A long shoot can be buried 20 cm (8 in) in the soil in spring or summer with just the tip still visible. The part which is deepest in the soil should be stripped of leaves and have a long slice cut off beneath one bud. Dust the cut with rooting powder and keep it open with a small wedge the size of a matchstick. The shoot can be anchored to the ground with pieces of wire bent into U-shapes.

Fill the hole with moistened soil mixed with peat and press this down lightly. Mark the rooting position with a stone. Prop up the end of the shoot that is sticking out above ground with another stone. Rooting will take place during the autumn. Do not separate the shoot from the mother plant until the following spring. Then cut it with a sharp spade.

Creating your own roses

This can be a fascinating adventure as you never know in advance exactly what the result is going to be. The aim when crossing plants is always to retain the best features of the two different roses which serve as the father and mother plants and unite them in a new variety. If you are lucky, you may obtain a rose with a completely new colour, a particularly handsome appearance and a subtle scent.

My tip: It is best to choose several plants as mother plants so that you have more available seed.

First step: Choose a father and mother rose. The flowers should be just beginning to open up.
Second step: Cut a flower stem approximately 15 cm (6 in) long from the father plant and stand it in water in a vase. Then choose a mother rose and pull off all the petals.
Third step: Using tweezers, remove all the stamens from the mother flower so that auto-pollination cannot occur. Use a magnifying glass if necessary. Place a paper bag over the flower to avoid any outside influence.
Fourth step: Remove the paper bag next day and have a look at the stigma. If they feel slightly sticky, they are ready to receive the pollen. Check, using a magnifying glass,

whether the father flower is ready to release the pollen. If so, gently wipe the stamens across the stigma of the mother flower.

Fifth step: Make sure that the yellow-orange pollen grains are adhering to the stigma. If not, repeat the pollination procedure.

Sixth step: Place a paper bag over the mother flower; it can be removed again after a week. If pollination was successful the base of the flower will swell and grow into a rosehip.

Seventh step: After a few months have passed, the rosehip can be snipped off. It should be ripe, but not yet wrinkled.

Eighth step: Bed the fruits in a dish containing damp peat and do not forget to attach a label with the names of the parents on it. Stand the container outside for the winter. Do not protect it from frost, as the seed should be frozen!

Ninth step: In the last month of spring, move the dish of rosehips inside. Extract the seeds from the hips and place them in a dish of water. Seeds which float will be infertile. Only choose seeds which sink to the bottom. Use seeding compost.

Tenth step: As soon as the young plants display their first tiny leaves, they should be pricked out in individual pots.

Small rose varieties were created for balconies and patios.

Grafting

Propagating from cuttings

From the middle of the last month of summer to the middle of the first month of autumn is the best time for this type of propagation. The rose shoots are just right for taking cuttings: they should be nice and firm but not completely woody.

First step: Cut off as many healthy shoots as you need. The cuttings should be at least 15 cm (6 in) long and about 30 cm (12 in) would be even better, as longer shoots have been observed to form roots more easily. Remove the flowers and the shoot tip above a cluster of five leaves (see illustration 1).

Second step: Remove all the leaves with the exception of the two lowest ones (see illustration 2).

Third step: Immerse each cutting first in water, then in rooting powder. Push the cuttings so far down into the soil that a finger-long piece with one bud is left poking out (see illustration 3). It is possible to insert the cutting into the ground in a sheltered spot in the garden in a mixture of garden soil, peat and sand or in pots of seeding compost. Place the cuttings in individual small pots or in groups of three in larger pots.

Fourth step: Press the cuttings down firmly and water them. If they are planted in pots, a transparent plastic bag should be pulled over the pot and the pots should be placed in a bright, but on no account sunny, position. If they are planted outside, make sure the cuttings do not become too wet or, conversely, dry out. Protect them with conifer branches before the start of frosty weather.

Fifth step: Rooting has taken place if new shoots begin to grow – often after eight to ten weeks. If the cuttings are in pots, now is the time to remove the plastic bags, separate the groups of three cuttings and place them in individual pots containing compost.

Budding a rose

Among the many methods of grafting roses, the following has proved itself time and again. Here a bud is removed from a chosen hybrid tea variety and tightly bound to the bare cambium of the wild stock so that it can continue growing there. The layer of tissue called cambium is situated immediately beneath the top layer of bark and consists of cells which are constantly replicating themselves. As plenty of warmth and light are required for this operation, it is best carried out towards the end of the second month/beginning of the third month of summer. Preparations for the procedure should have been made as early as the previous autumn or spring.

First step: Obtain the desired number of wild stock plants in spring or autumn and plant them in the positions in which they are intended to remain.

What you will need for budding a rose

- wild roses as stock for grafting (e.g. *Rosa canina* "Inermis", *Rosa canina* "Pfänders", *Rosa* "Laxa", *Rosa multiflora*, *Rosa pollmeriana*). You can obtain these from tree nurseries, rose growers and some garden centres;
- shoots of tea roses (hybrid tea cuttings);
- a budding knife (obtainable in the gardening trade);
- raffia or special rubber grafting bands (from garden centres etc.).

If there are no tree nurseries near you, just push a few cuttings of wild dog rose into the soil in the autumn. They will root very easily. In the spring, you should allow only the strongest main branch to remain.

Second step: During the second to third months of summer is the time for budding.

Propagation from cuttings

1. Take cuttings and remove flowers and shoot tips. The cuttings should be about 15 cm (6 in) or, better still, 30 cm (12 in) long.
2. Remove all leaves apart from the two topmost ones.
3. Dip the cutting in water, then in rooting powder and push it into the ground until only a finger-long piece is above ground.

Water the wild stock thoroughly a week beforehand. The ensuing flow of sap will enable you to loosen the bark more easily.

Third step: Expose the neck of the roots of the wild stock and wipe the soil away cleanly. In the case of standard and cascade roses, the grafting procedure should, of course, be carried out at the desired height, not as low as the neck of the root.

Fourth step: Thoroughly clean your hands and the budding knife with hot water and do not later touch the exposed cut surfaces with your hands. Cleanliness is the first pre-requisite for success.

Fifth step: Cut off one or several shoots from each rose that you would like to propagate. Remove all the thorns and leaves, the leaf stalks should remain (see illustration 1).

Sixth step: Find the fattest buds in the middle of each shoot. Using the razor-sharp budding knife, cut these off 2 cm (¾ in) above and below the bud together with a thin layer of bark which should also include a piece of the wood. Then remove the woody piece, leaving the bud undamaged (see illustration 2).

Seventh step: Now, using the budding knife, cut a long T into the bark of the neck of the root of the stock (see illustration 3). The cross of the T should reach halfway round the stem.

Eighth step: Gently loosen the flaps of bark of the T from the tissue underneath using the tapered end of the knife blade.

Ninth step: From above, gently push the piece of bark with the bud underneath the two flaps of bark in the T, so that the bud is peeking out at the top. The piece protruding above the T should be cut off (see illustration 4).

Tenth step: Tie gardener's raffia

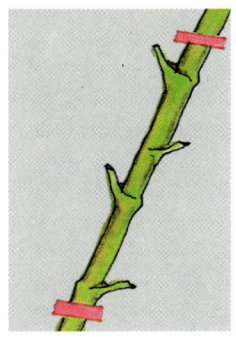

Grafting a rose

1. Cut a 30-cm (12 in) long, healthy shoot from the chosen rose.
2. Choose the fattest bud from the middle of the shoot and cut it out ovally, together with a piece of leaf stalk above and below the bud.
3. Cut a T-shape.
4. Push the grafting bud beneath the two flaps of bark.
5. Wind raffia around the grafting point. The bud must be exposed.

firmly around the grafting point or use a grafting band, covering the bark both above and below the piece of bark. Only the bud should be left poking out (see illustration 5).

Eleventh step: After the budding operation, the soil should be slightly heaped up around the budding point, but leaving the bud free.

Twelfth step: If the bud is still green after four weeks, is becoming fatter and the remaining leaf stalk drops off if touched gently, the stock and the bud should have fused together. Now cut the binding but do not yet remove it.

Thirteenth step: The following spring, cut off the crown of the wild stock 2 cm (¾ in) above the grafting point. Use your sharpest gardening secateurs for this procedure, as it is of immense importance for the future development of the rose that the crown is removed with a single, clean cut. Once the grafted buds have produced plenty of shoots, the shoot tips above the third and fourth leaves can be pinched out with your fingertips. This will promote the growth of new shoots.

A brief history of rose cultivation

Anecdotes and record breakers

Fossil evidence proves that the rose has existed for something like 40 million years. For thousands of years it was a common plant in the northern hemisphere. Around 1800, when the first attempts at crossing native European roses with Asian roses were successful, the rose gained greatly in variety and splendour.

A brief history of roses

During the course of human history, hardly any other flower has been so loved, cherished and sung about as the rose. In antiquity, it was considered to be a symbol of beauty and love. Christianity associated the rose with the delicate loveliness of the Virgin Mary; the Chinese worshipped the rose as a divine being. The first known artistic representations of roses are depicted on a fresco that is over 3,500 years old and can be found in the remains of a Minoan palace at Knossos on Crete. Sappho, a Greek poetess of the eighth century BC, is the first person known to have written a poem about the rose. Poets like Anacreon and Pindar followed her example. In the ancient garden culture of China roses were first planted in beds. Long before our period of reckoning, the Persians are known to have discovered how to make distilled rose water and extract rose oil, and it is thought that the cradle of the European rose

is to be sought in Persia. The Romans spent veritable fortunes on buying roses for decorative purposes for feasts and celebrations. They also used roses for medicinal purposes.

After the collapse of the Roman Empire, the rose seemed to be forgotten until Charlemagne revived an interest in it. Thereafter, the rose was cultivated, mainly for healing purposes, in monastery gardens. Famous artists such as Leonardo da Vinci, Michelangelo, Botticelli and Pieter Brueghel the Elder captured its beauty in marble and on canvas. Such famous physicians and botanists as Walafrid Strabo, Otto Brunfels, Leonhart Fuchs, Hieronymus Bosch, Tabernaemontanus, Clusius and Lonicerus all described the rose species known in their times.

In 1752, the first Asiatic rose, *Rosa chinensis*, was brought to Europe from Canton in China. This became the foundation plant for all the European garden roses.

Two hundred years of cultivating roses

"Modern" roses have actually been around no longer than this. To begin with, the East Asian roses were simply planted alongside the native ones and gardeners would wait to see if they cross-pollinated successfully. Finally, at the beginning of the nineteenth century, more scientific cultivation was undertaken. The French rose gardener Desportes had a total of 2,562 different roses in his catalogue in 1829. Then the first hybrid Chinese rose was created. From then on, the cultivation of new roses was unstoppable. France led the field, to be exact the French First Lady, Empress Josephine. She was responsible for speeding up the progress of the cultivation and crossing of roses as no other person before or after her. Her gardener, André Dupont, is thought to have been the first to cross-pollinate by hand. Her rose garden at Malmaison made the hobby of raising new rose cultivars popular all over Europe. In France itself, the first Remontant roses were created (1837), followed by hybrid teas (1867) and Polyantha roses in 1875. Later, these were overtaken by English and German cultivating activities. Countless varieties have been created all over the world to date, without the main aims of cultivation having changed a great deal. These are: good health, weather resistance, unusual flower colours and shapes and, of course, as many different scents as possible.

Roses in cuisine

What is pleasing to one's sense of smell ought to taste good too.

Rose punch: Sprinkle 300 g (10½ oz) scented, fresh rose petals with 150 g (5¼ oz) sugar, gently pour 10 ml Grand Marnier over them, cover and leave to soak in the refrigerator for an hour. Then pour 1 litre (¾ pt) dry white wine over this and allow it to stand in the refrigerator for another hour. Strain through a sieve and, shortly before serving, add chilled champagne. Allow a few fresh flower petals to float on top of the punch for decoration (serves about eight).

Roses for beauty and health

If you like making your own beauty preparations, you can create bath salts, creams, massage oils and perfumed shampoos or prepare a delicately flavoured tea out of scented roses from your garden. The flowers should be picked in the morning when the dew has dried, the petals carefully plucked off and spread out to dry on a clean tea cloth. Or they can be placed on a plate and dried at medium heat for one to two minutes in a microwave oven.

Rose tea: 1 handful of dried flower petals. Pour 0.75 litre (1¼ pt) of boiling water over the petals and leave this to draw for ten minutes. The tea can be drunk hot, sweetened with honey, or cold with lemon juice. The substances contained in the petals help to soothe the heart and fortify the liver and gall bladder.

Rose face tonic: Pour 100 ml organic white wine over 5 g rose petals and leave this in a dark container for two weeks. Strain the liquid well. Allow the rose wine to run through a coffee filter paper and mix it with 50 ml rose water bought from a chemist. Excellent for dry, sensitive skins.

The Gallica rose variety "Rosa mundi" grew in the twelfth century.

"Bonica 82", a modern, versatile rose of the eighties.

59

Index

Numbers in bold indicate pictures.

Index

Index

Useful addresses

Information and addresses of rose gardens, parks and rosariums can be obtained from the Royal Horticultural Society, Vincent Square, London SW1 2PE or the Royal National Rose Society, The Secretary, Bone Hill, Chiswell Green Lane, St Albans, Hertfordshire.

We recommend that queries should be accompanied by a stamped, self-addressed envelope.

Author's note

This book deals with the care of roses on balconies, patios and in the garden. Roses have thorns which can easily cause injuries. Always disinfect any wounds to prevent blood poisoning or infection, even it it is just a scratch. If in doubt, consult a doctor immediately. I strongly recommend that everyone who works regularly in the garden should have a tetanus vaccination for protection. Discuss this with your doctor. Please make absolutely sure that all plant protection agents, even biological ones, are kept in a safe place that is inaccessible to children and pets.

Cover photographs
Front cover: *Tea rose "Piroschka".*
Inside front cover: *Rosa gallica*
"Complicata".
Inside back cover; *Climbing roses in the*
rose garden on the island of Mainau,
Germany.
Back cover: *White climbing rose*
"Venusta Pendula".

Photographic acknowledgements
Apel: back cover; Eigstler: p. 25 top
right, bottom left, bottom centre, 26 top
left, 35; Fischer: p. 58, 59 top; Heitz: p.
10, 21, 22, 26 top right, bottom right,
29 left, 52/53; Jensen: p. 31 bottom
right; Kordes: p. 14, 25 top centre;
Mein Schöner Garten/Fischer: p. 54;
Mein Schöner Garten/Gross: p. 3,
16/17, 30 top right, 38; Mein Schöner
Garten/Rigby: p. 30 bottom left; Mein
Schöner Garten/Welsch:p. 11;
Pfletschinger: p. 46; Scherz: p. 44/45;
Stork: p. 8, 19; Strauss: inside front
cover, p. 20, 23 bottom centre, 30 top
left, bottom right; Welsch: p. 55;
Wetterwald: p. 32, 33 top right;
Reinhard: all other pictures.

This edition published 1995 by
Merehurst Limited
Ferry House, 51-57 Lacy Road,
Putney, London SW15 1PR

© 1990 Gräfe und Unzer GmbH, Munich

ISBN   1 85391 428 2

A catalogue record for this book is available from the British Library.

English text copyright ©
Merehurst Limited 1995
Translated by Astrid Mick
Edited by Lesley Young
Design and typesetting by
Cooper Wilson Design
Illustrations by Ushie Dorner
Printed in Singapore by Craft Print Pte Ltd